Finding
Your Plot
IN A PLOTLESS WORLD

We greatly appreciate your
commitment to the work of the
Lord. Love from Pastors Ralph &
Susan Olurotimi.
Provincial Pastors 2016.

Finding Your Plot

IN A PLOTLESS WORLD

{ A LITTLE DIRECTION }

DANIEL *de* ROULET

Brazos Press
Grand Rapids, Michigan

© 2007 by Daniel de Roulet

Published by Brazos Press
a division of Baker Publishing Group
P.O. Box 6287, Grand Rapids, MI 49516-6287
www.brazospress.com

Printed in the United States of America

Library of Congress Cataloging-in-Publication Data
Roulet, Daniel de, 1944–
    Finding your plot in a plotless world : a little direction / Daniel de Roulet.
        p.   cm.
    Includes bibliographical references.
    ISBN 10: 1-58743-120-3 (pbk.)
    ISBN 978-1-58743-120-3 (pbk.)
    1. Christian life. I. Title.
BV4501.3.R687 2007
248.4—dc22   2007004771

Contents

An Introduction to Plotlessness

My life can be summed up in three kinds of experiences: beauty, darkness, and nakedness.

Beauty seems to catch me napping. I don't seek it out; it breaks through to me in a desert night sky full of an impossible number of stars, or on a southern California beach when the Santa Ana winds blow offshore and flatten out the waves of the mighty Pacific, or in a pair of human eyes when I stop to really peer into them. Or in books.

I never liked books when I was young. One year my brother, twelve years my elder, came home from college over winter break with a list of books that he wanted me to read over the rest of the school year. This was well intentioned—perhaps he wanted to give me an opportunity he felt he had neglected growing up, or perhaps he saw potential in me and wanted to give me a head start. I nodded politely and perhaps even (though I doubt it) went on to pull out the hardbound copy of *David Copperfield* from the family bookshelf, but I was eight years old, and I found other things to do. Years later, when I was in graduate school and wondering why I seemed to have more trouble keeping up with the reading than my peers did, I ended up being tested for dyslexia and was not just a little dyslexic—I was off the charts. Actually, this gave me a certain peace with my childhood lack of reading and with my adult reading pace; ironically, I find some of my greatest reading joy (and beauty) now in Dickens's novels. But I don't need to tell you that there's beauty everywhere. It waits for us, like an ambush, despite those periods when it seems like beauty is nowhere to be found.

The periods when beauty is absent are darkness to me—not the dark beauty of the deep night sky that lets all those desert stars shine out in contrast. That's a romanticized kind of darkness that we wouldn't appreciate at all if it weren't for the lights. I'm thinking about an absence of light: numbness, or a world turned gray, or the way we feel when we cry tears that bring no catharsis to our souls. I have seen this darkness in my dad's untimely death, when my son was given a serious diagnosis, or whenever the rug was pulled out from under whatever sense of plot I had in this life, when I felt like I had been blindsided, and getting up off the ground was no fun at all. J. Hillis Miller, a professor at the university I attended, wrote a book about literature in the nineteenth century that describes this sort of experience. He believed that the Victorian era was a time when the rug of meaning had been pulled out from under all our feet in the Western world, when the old answers faced too many challenges. Miller believed that many pieces of Victorian literature were examples of people desperately trying to rebuild the bridges that had fallen down between themselves and what gave life meaning. Novels tried to battle what it felt like to be looking for plot in a suddenly plotless world.

> I'm thinking about an absence of light: numbness, or a world turned gray, or the way we feel when we cry tears that bring no catharsis to our souls.

Nakedness is the third kind of experience. When I was a young professor, I was asked to give the sermon at our graduation baccalaureate service in a beautiful basilica on the north side of Chicago, in front of our students and their guests—about 3,000 people in all. I was terrified. One of my colleagues advised me to imagine that my audience was naked. I'm assuming she wanted me to not imagine myself naked along with them, because if you're the only one in the room wearing clothes, then there's a sense of power over the rest of the folks.

But nakedness can work both ways. There are times when, metaphorically, everyone else is dressed and you're the only naked one present. I now attend a very large church—I think it's larger than the desert town where I attended high school—that has everything you could hope for. My children like the youth program so much that they actually want to attend church, and they seem to listen to and digest what they hear. There are endless opportunities to serve others, and we have a roster of pastors who can all teach, who all have their own styles, and who speak about issues of substance. I feel rich at church. And rich people usually don't find themselves involuntarily naked.

So one Sunday I went to church and sat far in the back where I could be safe and just observe. My wife was out of town visiting relatives, and my children were at their own service, so I was Mr. Incognito for the day. The pastor was one of the "fill-in" guys, one who gets to preach when the big boys are out of town, or on the Sundays between the completion of one sermon series and the beginning of the next. He decided to teach about judgment (a topic that excites me only about as much as the prospect of hearing a sermon on tithing—I want to inconspicuously leave, or I want to catch up on my letter writing). But he did not want to talk about God's judgment of us; instead, he wanted to talk about our fascination with judging other people and our total lack of interest in applying the same tactics to ourselves. He used Jesus's very simple story of the man who tries to remove an annoying speck of dust from his friend's eye while apparently not noticing that he has a log stuck in his own. Listening to the sermon was like falling into the deep end of the pool and endlessly sinking—not growing short of breath, but just wondering when I was going to hit bottom. I looked around the church. Most of my fellow congregants weren't paying a lot of attention. They sat comfortably in their Sunday finest while I felt caught, enthralled and personally stricken because of who I am, naked as a baby. The pastor told us that God wanted us to understand this problem we have, not because he is out to get us, but because of how much he cares about what will happen to us, and who we will become, if we don't understand.

Writers call these epiphany moments: when the whole world becomes clear, when the good things we have and our enormous failures all raise their hands and then stand up to be counted. God, and whoever else is involved, and I myself see me for exactly who I am. And God, and if I'm lucky, whoever else is involved, and maybe even I myself love me anyway and help me to change. All of the things I thought were important—all the plots I had written for my own life—fade away in these experiences.

I wish that the times of beauty would last forever, or at least be the majority of life, but they don't and they're not. I'm glad the times of darkness don't come even more often then they do. I once had a cat that had some serious psychological problems: he chose to sleep in the tree in the backyard to protect him from what he saw as an endlessly threatening world. If darkness dominated life more than it does—and it does plenty already, thank you—then I'd never come out of the tree, so to speak. Nakedness needs to happen. As Job said, "Naked I came from my mother's womb, and naked I will depart" (Job 1:21). It's no use fooling ourselves about who we are, even though as a species we're very good at being preoccupied with clothes.

In the midst of these three kinds of episodes, we tell each other stories to try to sort out life, to find plot and meaning in a world that can seem plotless. I have found that God is interested in stories as well: the Bible is full of disarming accounts of people's lives and stories like the one Jesus told about the speck and the log. This book looks at the stories we tell in our own lives and through literature, and the stories that God tells back to us through the Bible. It starts out with moments in life in which we lose our plots, and ends with the times in which we find them. I'm telling my stories here of when my life has seemed plotless and of how I found my plot again; I hope they offer you a little direction in sorting out your own.

Telling Our Stories,
Eclipses and All

At eight years old, I was ready for Little League baseball season to begin. In fact, I had been ready since Christmas. But that April in New Jersey was especially cold and windy, as if spring didn't want to arrive. Snow stayed piled in the shadows of the trees. The few green stalks that poked through the ground seemed stunted in their growth.

On the morning after my father and I had a serious conversation, I sat alone on the back porch—its glass storm windows still in place—watching wild white clouds fly across the pale sky in which the light of springtime had not yet been formed. My father had told me that he was going to Houston for an operation, and that my mother would be going, too. I don't remember the details of the arrangements while they were gone—my sister was sixteen, and I imagine that people from church brought us meals and checked in. It's amazing what one remembers, and after so many years, one wonders if the memories are true. But I clearly remember three things about those weeks.

First, my sister invited her boyfriend over for dinner, and she spent several hours late one afternoon, in anticipation of her boyfriend's arrival, cooking—or rather, burning. What had been steaks filled the kitchen with a fine outdoor barbeque odor, and she ran around the house opening storm windows, letting the cold night air in, transforming the house by the time of the boyfriend's arrival from warm and smoky to cold and smoky.

I also remember that my sister adopted a kitten in my parents' absence. As far back as I could remember my sister had picked up stray pets as a way of life. They consistently loved her and always disrupted the house—dogs that refused to behave, cats that tried to lord it over the dog. Thank goodness she didn't like birds. This cat, a small black and white furball, quickly developed a habit of hiding under the living room sofa and pouncing on anyone who passed. At times he went for the ankles; at other times he hung from your belt. A year later, when we were selling the house, he was particularly unpleasant to a woman who had outbid a nice young couple. No one liked her. The cat ran her stockings; I think he drew blood, and she decided not to buy. So, in the time my parents were away in Houston, I mainly remember a cantankerous kitten bounding fearlessly through a house in which a hint of burnt steak smell had worked its way into the fabric of the furniture and the carpet.

Finally, though, I remember one morning, and I will remember it as long as I live. I had been sleeping in my parents' empty room in their absence, at the front of the house, tucking myself close against the wall and trying not to watch the ghostly patterns that passing car headlights made on the walls. The morning dawned warmer, cloudy, and thundering. I looked outside my window into the clouds and heard a low rumble of thunder, like God's own voice rocking across the morning air, and I knew—deep inside me, without a doubt. So I put on my slippers and walked to the bedroom window and looked into the driveway to find two unfamiliar cars parked there. Then I walked into the kitchen and saw two women from our church sitting at the breakfast table, crying. I walked over to them, and they told me that my father had passed away after the operation and that I was the man of the house now and that I would have to be strong for my sister and my mother. I was eight and, of course, not feeling particularly strong about anything.

We sold the house later that year and moved west to be with my mother's relatives. The Lutheran church we attended in the small desert town was nothing like the church we had left. This one was spare: chairs in the sanctuary instead of pews, a one-level Sunday school wing that looked and felt temporary; a courtyard separated the two buildings in which the lawn and small trees seemed to be locked in a losing battle with the heat and the desert wind. I had become a stranger, and when the other kids in Sunday school asked me why I had a mother but no father, sometimes I didn't have the words to answer, and sometimes, when the words came, the kids who had asked could not adequately respond. My brother, now graduated from college, and my sister, a high-schooler quite unhappy with having been uprooted from all she had known, had been drifting away from church life for some time. They had wondered rather openly about the need they saw in parishioners to put on church faces, about their abilities to talk about God's grace and power and their inabilities to confess and confront hardships and failings and weaknesses. After we had moved west, those were the things we needed to talk about. We needed to tell stories that didn't seem to fit into the brighter, hopeful narratives of Sunday morning. The best metaphor I can muster is that my life felt at that moment like a solar eclipse: the sun was hidden, the light grew odd, and the very world changed.

People who have experienced an eclipse come away with a similar set of descriptions: a sudden realization that everything around you has become the wrong color, a feel of chill in the air, a shimmering of shadows, a sudden quiet as even birds realize that something has gone wrong. That is how my father's death affected my family: when we left New Jersey and moved to the desert of California, I think I saw that move as an exile of sorts, a continuing eclipse from which the sun refused to emerge for a long while. I would like to say that eight or nine years old is a little early to experience life's eclipses, except that in my career as a teacher I have come to see it almost as a rule rather than an exception in my students: parents divorce, fathers or mothers die, children are removed from abusive situations, young women in particular, barely having entered their teens, feel such pressure from our culture to be perfect that they experience eating disorders, alcohol and drug abuse, or sexual recklessness as a means of obtaining a sense of physical comfort and stability. Who at eight or nine, thirteen or sixteen—even at twenty or thirty or forty—is equipped to navigate landscapes that have gone so askew?

> We needed to tell stories that didn't seem to fit into the brighter, hopeful narratives of Sunday morning.

We talk in our churches about the need to minister to the church of the twenty-first century, to find ways to keep the church relevant in a world in which almost daily there seems to be a greater and greater cultural divide between the standards of the Christian life and popular culture. But perhaps the issue is not how well our churches do in upholding values and protesting cultural trends, but simply how well they hear and accept stories that don't speak of victory but of trial or defeat. How well do we avoid the cosmetic tones of Sunday morning and instead convince our visitors and even our church members that God understands human difficulty and failure? Amazingly enough, the Bible—the food of the church—is full of such stories, but we shy away from telling them.

The lives of the people who fill the pages of the Hebrew scriptures, and Jesus's stories in the New Testament, tell about a life full of eclipses. Our best plans are interrupted by the realities of our fallen world, and during those times it is difficult to discern God's plans for us—if anything, our sense of a plotted life seems interrupted at best. To deny these eclipses removes a portion of our humanity in the eyes of our neighbors; they look at us as Christian phonies, and they wait for the truth to come out. Sometimes God reaches us in the depths of our despair, but often, as the Bible itself testifies, we are left for a time with a sense of darkness and disorder, even if deep in our hearts we know that God is still there and working in our lives. Why don't we talk so well at church about these stories?

Moments of Eclipse and Authenticity

During a recent November I went to Atlanta for a literary conference. The keynote speaker, and the subject of many of the sessions, was to be Lee Smith, a Virginia native and author of three collections of short stories and eleven novels. That she was to be the focus of a literary conference is in itself unusual—Smith, and a growing generation of southern women writers, many of whom she has mentored, don't get a lot of press from book critics. Her books are not "literary novels" in the sense of language and theme; the voices of the narrators are often unsophisticated, more the voices of some women who have grown up and remained in the rural South than, as with Flannery O'Connor's characters, of those who have returned educated from the North to find their former neighbors wanting. What fascinated me about Smith's stories when I first encountered them were their dangerously Christian themes: an early novel about a young woman's encounter with the Holy Spirit, a short story in which a well-to-do retiree has a religious experience one summer afternoon on a North Carolina beach, much to the dismay of her grown children. What continued to draw me in was her ability to tell a story, the authenticity of her characters, and my curiosity over both the remnants of Christian identity and fewer mentions of Christian faith that emerge over time in her narratives.

When I arrived at the conference, sadness and disappointment were palpable among the participants. Lee Smith would not be attending; she had cancelled because, two weeks earlier, she had buried her son. Smith has spent the latter part of her career giving herself to people—working in adult literacy projects, encouraging the voiceless to tell their stories, bringing to light oral histories and the music of the South's mountain communities, teaching writing, generously reading her writing and conducting interviews in a number of venues, working to create avenues for women's voices to be heard. When her hometown of Grundy, Virginia, experienced a forced relocation to higher ground because of a flood, Smith organized a local oral history project to preserve the memory of what Grundy once was.

Many of these themes were well represented at the conference's smaller sessions, but what was missing was any sense of Smith's spiritual life and themes. The conference was not opposed to such themes per se—there were sessions on spirituality in African American southern fiction, and I read a paper on eighteenth-century Methodism. When I left the conference, taking the train back to the airport, I was left to wonder what had gone wrong. Lee Smith is all about storytelling, and somehow the stories she has told should be of interest to any human—but the themes of love and loss, adventure and middle age, loyalty and infidelity, celebrations and life's eclipses, have not made it into the reading circles of the Christian community. This is especially strange given the concerns of some of her most accomplished works.

"Mrs. Darcy Meets the Blue-Eyed Stranger at the Beach," winner of the O. Henry Award for short fiction, is the centerpiece of Smith's first collection of stories, *Cakewalk*. The story's protagonist, Lolly Darcy, is a recent widow who is joined at the family summer home on the North Carolina beach by her three grown daughters, sons-in-law, and grandchildren. The daughters are concerned about their mother's dotage since their father's death. Trixie, the oldest, finds herself with the uncomfortable prospect of becoming a mother to her mother; Maria, a psychologist married to another psychologist, is soon to have marital problems; and Ginny, the youngest, is in therapy herself and is working out her own family angst. The Darcy family is used to a life based on keeping up appearances, and Mrs. Darcy, since the death of her husband, simply isn't playing along. The woman who once wouldn't dream of a family meal without fine china, fine food, perfect dress, and matching behavior is now trailing around the summer house in flip-flops and a housecoat. There is dust on everything, and the refrigerator is filled with previously unacceptable items: Coca-Colas, Hawaiian Punch, frozen pizzas. She refuses to socialize, has given up volunteer work, and has neglected even her hobbies and usual social outlets. Her only friend is her beach neighbor, Margaret. As the children share concerns together over their mother on the beach, suddenly all action is stopped by the appearance of a double rainbow, the first in anyone's memory. Mrs. Darcy comes out onto the porch:

She raised her arms suddenly, stretching them up and out towards the rainbows. "Ai-yi-yi!" she wailed loudly. "Yi-yi-yi!" Mrs. Darcy stood transfixed, then fell forward onto the sandy deck in a dead faint. (142)

After this incident, the children's concern evolves into panic. They are due back in the city, back to their various scheduled lives, but what to do about their mother? To make matters worse, Mrs. Darcy refuses to see a doctor, spends her time lying amidst pillows on a daybed, and yet seems to have taken on what Smith describes as a "new, luminous quality." Mrs. Darcy enthusiastically tells her children that during the episode of the double rainbow, she suddenly experienced "this presence" that filled her up "until [she] was floating." Then she saw a long-haired, blue-eyed man, wearing a long white garment, who stretched out his arms and called her by name.

We, and the children themselves, are not sure what to make of this episode. Has Lolly had a stroke? Is she ready for a nursing home? But what of this new sense of happiness and energy (she even takes a swim in the ocean) after the event she describes? Is Smith poking fun at religious experience? As one of the characters states, "I think we have to proceed very carefully here."

But Lolly improves, no longer mentions the blue-eyed stranger, and seems even to be able to speak of her late husband with a casual warmth. She becomes more communicative and acquiesces to her eldest daughter's parental directives, even to the point of trying out children's art projects as a hobby. All are surprised when Ginny, the troubled youngest child, offers to stay at the beach house to keep an eye on Mrs. Darcy as the others retreat to the city. Life seems to be returning to normal.

So Ginny goes out for the evening, and Mrs. Darcy calls her friend Margaret, who brings along another friend who cannot be cured by doctors, whose pain in her shoulder doesn't allow her to sleep. Mrs. Darcy touches her, and later in the evening the friend is described as completely healed and radiant. Apparently, Margaret brought her around because, earlier, Mrs. Darcy had healed her too. Mrs. Darcy refuses the woman's offer of payment:

"It's not me at all," Lolly tells them. "I'm just an agent, an intermediary."

The story ends without an explanation for Lolly's newfound gifts, just an assurance of their effectiveness.

Perhaps if such episodes in Smith's work were truly isolated, they could be easily dismissed as a passing interest in local mountain color—the religious experiences of backwoods churches and storefronts. But the central story—really a novella—in her second collection of short fiction, *Me and My Baby View the Eclipse,* is mentioned by Smith as her most autobiographical.

Karen, the young teenaged narrator of "Tongues of Fire" finds herself in the midst of a family crisis. Her mother is most concerned about how she and the family will appear in the eyes of interested neighbors as her father slides into a nervous breakdown. Moreover, he has the "nerve" to have his breakdown on the putting green of the family's country club, in full view of all the other members dining in the clubhouse. Karen meanwhile takes an interest in experiential Christianity, the faith of the lower social classes of her town. Although in her initial encounter it is unclear whether she is more spiritually or physically attracted to a young Methodist preacher, subsequently she begins to sneak out to a friend's country church, in which she is baptized. Then, at a summer church camp for Episcopalians (her mother's choice—a way of getting Karen back onto the right social track), Karen develops a fever and has a religious experience. Her cabin fills with a warm light, and she runs onto the assembly stage where, in front of aghast counselors and fellow campers, she begins to speak in tongues. She is, of course, sent home.

Karen's life, like Lolly's, returns to normal. She takes ribbing from her classmates about her newfound gift and does not respond. She grows up and loses her religious fervor that once encouraged her to "pray without ceasing." And yet at the story's end, the narrator, now an adult, states that there are times when in the quiet of the day she hears the voice of God and responds, as did the prophets of old, "Here I am, Lord."

Thus does a portion of Smith's fiction seem to portray an interesting countercultural group in the contemporary United States: those whose Christian faith, vibrant and effective, marginalizes them from the socially acceptable avenues of spiritual expression. The mainstream Christianity expressed in the stories is one of social assimilation. But if these characters of faith, who apparently share some elements of Smith's own life, are so present and central in some of her work, why are the stories not embraced by people of faith? Why do mentions of effective religious community fade as Smith's work progresses? The answer seems to be in one of Smith's most dominant symbols: the eclipse, a time when life as we know it should be has been turned upside down. The sun has been blocked, the world is seen through an unnatural light, and all that we profess and live by is put to the test. Any religious community can claim authenticity when life goes well, but how do its members treat one another when the vision for how life should be, either corporately or individually, goes awry?

Smith's fiction is as complicated as life itself, and she is most critical of those people or organizations that would deny such complications. To shy away from such difficulties is to send a message that God and God's people are somehow afraid of the problems of humanity—or worse, immune to them. While the motives of Smith's characters, be they religiously inclined or not, are often difficult to sort out, they are more often driven at the root by authenticity. One of her narrators who writes a Christian advice column for the local small-town paper confesses her own complications—she sometimes does not wish her readers well, she has in the past engaged in an affair that would have scandalized her fellow church members, and she does not even always understand herself! Smith's protagonists divorce, or have affairs, or have any number of eclipses in which, for an episode, life is no longer as it should be, but she presents these episodes as facts of life.

One of her most compelling short stories, "Bob, a Dog," is the story of Cheryl, who comes down the stairs holding a basket of laundry one morning only to hear the pronouncement of her husband, darkly framed in the doorway like the moon slipping in front of the sun, that he has decided that he needs a "new life." His notion of new life is escape from responsibility—an affair—and Cheryl is left with the problems of children and an aging mother, making ends meet financially, and figuring out just who she is as her husband moves in with a self-proclaimed feminist professor at a local college. Bob is a dog who is not a particularly helpful presence in Cheryl's time of need and exacerbates the family's problems by constantly making messes in the house and, after his exile to the backyard, digging his way out of an increasingly complicated pen and ruining the neighbors' lawns. Bob, like life's problems, cannot be kept in neat categories, and cannot be kept from the view of the neighbors. In fact, as time goes on, the facade becomes comical.

The most telling, I think, of Smith's stories in the collection is a no-holds-barred satire on supermarket romances, called "Desire on Domino Island." This story most directly challenges the stereotypical Christian community that Smith's characters find less and less attractive as her career progresses. Smith begins the story by stepping out of the realm of fiction, explaining a friend's desire to take a break from writing a doctoral dissertation in order to try writing a romance novel. In receiving the writers' guidelines from the publisher, both Smith and her friend seem amused and bemused by the strictures imposed: the heroine must be a virgin, the man (upon whom no such restrictions are placed) must be constructed to fit a certain physical type, the other characters must be minor (so as to not detract from the hero and heroine), and life must be free of "complications," included in which are children! The message sent by the guidelines is that life must follow a precise plot; any departures from how life in romances should go will upset the reader and result in an unsuccessful book.

When I think of my sister and brother, who effectively left the church during their teen years, I realize that their decisions were complicated ones. But I also wonder if they saw an organization that accepted few deviations from the agreed-upon "plot" of the Christian life. Smith's friend finished and submitted her romance novel, but it was rejected, Smith claims, because it contained two unacceptable elements: symbolism and semicolons.

"Desire on Domino Island," after Smith's introductory remarks, is a condensed version of her own "attempt" at a romance novel. Despite mostly adhering to the guidelines, Smith's characters and the story itself simply cannot contain themselves, and it is from this that the satire on the romance form ensues. Jennifer Maidenfern, the orphaned heroine, seeks the home left to her on the island and encounters Rock Cliff, our paperback romance hero with whom, almost against her will, she falls in love. Other characters color the story but do not take away from the focus on Jennifer and Rock. The prescribed plot rolls on, but

Smith cannot bring herself to fully write the story: chapter 8, for example, is allocated only a little more than two lines. Finally, Smith directly imposes her critique at the romance's end. Jennifer and Rock "embrace as, behind them, the sun rises out of the sea." Smith writes to finish the story:

> And that's it! I shade my eyes against the brightness of this sun, the glare off the water, but in vain: all I can see is the silhouette. Jennifer and Rock have nothing, nothing left—no faces, no bodies, not to mention fear or pain or children, joy or memory or loss—nothing but these flat black shapes against the tropic sky. (135)

To "accept life" but deny the very qualities that make it human would leave us with only a two-dimensional story. And here it is: the flat black story of Jennifer and Rock that eclipses life's light, leaving us readers with nothing to relate to or care about.

If, as Christians, we make the error of believing that a Christian life is one in which we present only successes, and that we must keep our human failures away from the view of the neighbors, then are we certain we are presenting God's plot for life and the authenticity of our own? If for a moment we can bring Lee Smith's stories into conversation with God's own stories from the Bible, we will see a view of life in which such questions and their complications are embraced, even in the life of a man "after God's own heart."

Authenticity in the Old Testament

> Who am I, O Sovereign Lord, and what is my family, that you have brought me this far? . . . How great you are, O Sovereign Lord! There is no one like you . . . (2 Sam. 7:18, 22)

The story has always served this function, I believe, from the beginning of time. In the telling of it, we discover who we are, why we exist, what we should do. It brings order and delight. (Lee Smith, "In Her Own Words," 1)

Imagine yourself as a flannel-board character. You have seen these in your child's preschool, or perhaps you remember them from a Sunday school lesson: Noah and the ark and the animals, two by two, or Joseph and his coat of many colors. Like Smith's characters in "Desire on Domino Island," flannel-board characters are two-dimensional: we can dress Joseph or Noah up, but their stories, confined to the board, really have no place to go. What do we know of Noah's emotions as he waits for the flood? What of Joseph's thoughts after the coat is torn and he is sold by his brothers into slavery?

When my oldest son was in first grade, he was asked what his father did for a living, and he answered, "My dad reads books and drinks coffee." So my flannel-board self probably would be a man in a professorial sports jacket; my accessories would be a comfortable chair, a stack of books, and a cup of coffee. It would reduce me to a caricature.

My guess is that one of the least flannel-boarded lives in the Old Testament would be that of David, the second king of Israel. Indeed, unless one settles for the young David as shepherd or slayer of Goliath, I shudder to think what episodes of David's adult life could be used for Sunday school. One of the lives recorded in most detail in the Bible, really one of God's longest and most detailed stories, is that of David—king of Israel, warrior, man of God—whose life leaves no room for keeping up appearances. The stories that God tells are not flannel-boarded Sunday school lessons; instead, they are filled with beauty, and darkness, and nakedness.

David's story tells the life of a man whose heart is given to God in the midst of a litany of both victories and troubles. Is it curious to any other readers of the Bible that David, king of Israel, is described as "a man after God's own heart"? That description does not apply to his many failures: his most famous encounter with Bathsheba and the ordered murder of her husband as David attempts to cover his sin; the disastrous rebellion of his children, especially that of Absalom; his repeated exile from his own kingdom; the refusal of God to allow David to build the temple because of the blood on David's hands. We are more likely to look at David's shining moments of faith, and rightly so, in order to discern the kinship of his heart and God's. We remember the boy who takes on Goliath when the best fighters and even the king of Israel seemed afraid to do so. This David pronounced his faith in songs, in dancing, in acts of bravery and sacrifice. But perhaps another element, alongside that faith, placed him steadfastly in God's company and witnessed to the kind of God he had found. If this is true, then we have hope for ourselves, and quite a story to tell our neighbors as we all, together as humans, share lives dotted with eclipses.

Unless one reads the story of his life straight through, one doesn't get a good enough sense of the kind of life David led. One thinks of him as the favored son, or the glorious king of Israel who through battle and rule put the nation together. Take a look, however, at a brief outline of the plot of David's life:

1. He is anointed king by God's prophet over his older brothers, much to their disapproval and jealousy.
2. His first task, post-anointment and pre-coronation, is to play a harp to calm the current king (Saul), who is afflicted by a demon.

3. He then volunteers to kill Goliath, the champion of the opposing army, whom even the most experienced fighting men of Israel would not challenge.

4. King Saul becomes jealous of David and tries to kill him with a spear as he sings.

5. Saul plots David's death: it is to take place in battle.

6. Saul orders his son and his servants to kill David.

7. David flees the kingdom because of Saul's death threats and is forced to feign madness to avoid death at the hands of another ruler.

8. Saul, after killing the priests of Israel for helping David, personally leads his men against David.

9. David again removes himself from the kingdom.

10. Saul and his son Jonathan, David's great friend, die in battle.

11. David enters a kingdom embroiled in civil war and retribution.

12. David enters a period of blessing and victory.

13. Upon solidifying his power, David commits adultery with Bathsheba and then has her husband killed.

14. The son of their union dies soon after his birth.

15. Incest and murder occur among David's children.

16. David's son Absalom attempts to take his father's throne.

17. David again flees his kingdom.

18. Against David's orders, his military commander kills Absalom.

19. David sins against God by counting his armed forces (trusting in his own strength rather than in God), and his kingdom is greatly punished as a result.

20. David is told by God that he cannot build the temple because of the bloodshed caused by his hands.

21. Another of David's sons tries to take his throne.

22. David establishes his son Solomon (his son by Bathsheba) as his heir.

At least two observations are noteworthy in examining this list. First, what kind of life is this for someone who claims to have found God's favor? If someone is in trouble and is seeking God as a release from those troubles, what message will that person find here? But more importantly, David's life with God is not a life in which suddenly everything goes well—it is instead a life in which David prevails despite horrific odds; it is an authentic human life in which God refuses to abandon him. The message of God's story in the life of David is best seen in the king of Israel's darkest moments.

The account of King David's adultery with Bathsheba is probably one of the best-known episodes of the Old Testament. What is less known is the context, the full story. David's great failure occurs at the end of a string of victories. When I teach drama in introductory literature classes, we discuss the Greek notion of the tragic hero. Such a hero, according to Aristotle, has a problem: *hubris* (or *hybris*). *Hubris* is usually translated as "excessive pride," but a fuller definition is more useful. It is the sort of pride common to those people who experience tremendous, and often unlooked-for, success. The Greeks' understanding of an effective and tragic hero is a person who—because of talent, fortune, and blessing—works his or her way up from a common place to one of great respect. Our best examples today could be American presidents—a Richard Nixon, who was the son of a poor and strict Quaker family, or a Bill Clinton, the child of a broken home. Each experiences a road, beset with some failures, that eventually leads to great public success. However, as we humans achieve success, we tend to forget about the parts of the equation involving blessing and good fortune and focus only on our talents. As we stand in front of a series of increasingly large crowds of admirers, we begin to believe our own press clippings. And as we do so, we believe that we are special, set apart—we mistakenly believe that the rules that apply to the rest of the universe do not apply to us.

David, the youngest son of a shepherd, was taken by God out of a life of obscurity as a replacement for a king who had failed. Yes, God saw something in David's heart that earned his notice, but David would be nowhere without God's action. The expression "There but for the grace of God go I" is not a put-down of others, but a reminder that believers are made of the same materials as everyone else, and that it is only God's action—not some inherent talent—that accounts for our success. After a series of horrible trials (see the list above), David enters into a time of life filled with victory and success. His victories in battle are greeted by the cry of the people, "Saul has slain his thousands, and David his tens of thousands" (1 Sam. 29:5), a comparison that does not elude King Saul. After the chaos of transition, David begins to enjoy success as king. When he is thirty years old, the people crown him king, calling him one of them, "our own flesh and blood." He conquers a fortress city (Jerusalem) thought to be unconquerable. He defeats long-standing enemies of his people. He brings the Ark of the Covenant, the vehicle and place of God's presence, into Jerusalem to dwell among the people of Israel. The borders of Israel expand under God's blessing and David's leading of a series of military victories. David blesses the last remaining son of the house of Saul in a gesture of reconciliation and unity within the kingdom. His triumph over the army of the neighboring Ammonites is particularly impressive. Near this time David responds with a heartfelt piety, saying,

Who am I, O Sovereign LORD, and what is my family, that you have brought me this far? (2 Sam. 7:18)

Then, as David's successes and his hubris grow, he encounters Bathsheba.

On a spring evening, David, on the rooftop of his palace, looks down and sees Bathsheba bathing. He is taken with her, desires to sleep with her, and is immediately told that she is married. Nonetheless, he carries out his desires, and Bathsheba becomes pregnant with the king's child. Instead of confessing his sin, David decides to try to keep up appearances, and so he enters into a long and awful period of deception. He brings her husband home from war so that the husband, Uriah, will sleep with his wife and think that she is pregnant by him. But Uriah, denying special treatment and in loyalty to those with whom he fights, refuses. David then conspires with his commander, Joab, to have Uriah placed in the front lines and abandoned in battle. This plan succeeds, and David brings Bathsheba, now a widow, to the palace to be one of his wives. God responds through his prophet Nathan, who confronts David over his sin, telling the king a parable of a rich man who, despite his plenty, takes away the only possession a poor man has.

> There were two men in a certain town, one rich and the other poor. The rich man had a very large number of sheep and cattle, but the poor man had nothing except one little ewe lamb he had bought. He raised it, and it grew up with him and his children. It shared his food, drank from his cup and even slept in his arms. It was like a daughter to him.
>
> Now a traveler came to the rich man, but the rich man refrained from taking one of his own sheep or cattle to prepare a meal for the traveler who had come to him. Instead, he took the ewe lamb that belonged to the poor man and prepared it for the one who had come to him. (2 Sam. 12:1–4)

After David responds to the story by saying, "The man who did this deserves to die!" (2 Sam. 12:5), Nathan retorts that David is the very man—he, in his plenty and unchecked desire, believing that the rules of the universe do not apply to someone as special as himself, has taken away all that Uriah had, and then killed him to conceal his crime.

David's sin is all too human in its roots, but those on the grand stage commit sin that affects a grand scope. Nathan responds:

> This is what the LORD, the God of Israel, says: "I anointed you king over Israel, and I delivered you from the hand of Saul. I gave your master's house to you, and your master's wives into your arms. I gave you the house of Israel and Judah. And if all this had been too little, I would have given you even more. Why did you despise the word of the LORD by doing what is evil in his eyes? You struck down Uriah the Hittite with the sword and took his wife to be your own. You killed him with the sword of the Ammonites. Now, therefore, the sword will never depart from your house, because you despised me and took the wife of Uriah the Hittite to be your own." (2 Sam. 12: 7–10)

David's own home is subsequently filled with trouble, and his kingdom enters a period of bloodshed and rebellion that really never leave it. Yet David's reaction is of great note. One of the results of his sin is the death of the child born to Bathsheba out of wedlock. During the time of the child's illness, David pleads for the child, but the innocent child dies. David's behavior is explained as follows:

> "While the child was alive, I fasted and wept. I thought, 'Who knows? The LORD may be gracious to me and let the child live.' But now that he is dead, why should I fast? Can I bring him back again? I will go to him, but he will not return to me."
>
> Then David comforted his wife Bathsheba, and he went to her and lay with her. She gave birth to a son, and they named him Solomon. The LORD loved him . . . (2 Sam. 12:22–24)

This is a deeply difficult story—one that is disarmingly honest. David experiences a myriad of eclipses in his life where the world seems to have turned upside down; in this case, the eclipse is of his own doing. The message to the believer, however, is not "I am now sinless" or "I am now without troubles," but "I have entered into a relationship with a God who stays with me through my troubles and despite my sins—and they have been and are very real—and I am now called to help others in trouble and to end the deception and to make right my sins." In this story of David, God draws him with no concern of keeping up appearances, and the result is disturbing. But we also see a God who is capable of making goodness out of disaster. Solomon will rule in ways David could not. And, in his faith, David knows that someday he will see his dead son again, in a place beyond this life where all will be made as it should be.

Sharing Our Eclipses

I have a strange idea for what I wish small groups or Bible studies at church would be. Don't get me wrong: I have seen such gatherings be places of great honesty and transparency; more often, however, I have experienced them as places in which we talk about our problems but not our sins, and as places where the "we" involved feel a lot of pressure to agree with each other and to be very much alike, even if we are not. At their worst, church small groups drive me crazy; at my worst, I'm a solid contributor to the problem. Here's an idea: I wish I were in a small group with people in my church and Lee Smith. Chances are the churchgoers would spend a lot of time feeling uncomfortable or worrying about Lee's salvation, but I think we believers would have a lot to learn from her company.

I think back now to the conference at which I hoped to meet Lee Smith. As I rode the train back to the Atlanta airport after the final session, I was preoccupied with eclipses. We live in a world where sometimes fathers and mothers bury their sons, where young men and women rebel against their families and do not come home, where we make mistakes and try like Bob the dog to cover them, hoping no one will notice those fresh markings where we buried the bone.

We spend a large percentage of our energy keeping up appearances. Such a task is exhausting. Why not, in allowing God's stories to answer our own, offer an alternative? Christians are called by their very name to be "little Christs" living real lives in plain view, small examples of the incarnation that God himself chose. He did not stay above the world, but he entered into it, was born in a place without distinction, and became intimate from the first with the troubles of his times. What I would like church to be like is a meeting place of authenticity, in which everyone, believer and nonbeliever alike, is acknowledged to be human and flawed and in need of a God who can do something about it—and we love one another with no strings attached.

> What I would like church to be like is a meeting place of authenticity, in which everyone, believer and nonbeliever alike, is acknowledged to be human and flawed and in need of a God who can do something about it—and we love one another with no strings attached.

To do any less, to pretend to live those two-dimensional dimestore-romance lives in which eclipses do not occur, cheapens the message of the gospel and drives people away from the kingdom of God.

If Lee Smith had been in Atlanta that weekend, I suspect I would have had the opportunity to sit in the presence of someone quite honest about life's episodes of plotlessness—someone who does not edit them into two-dimensional flatness. I wish that my own life, with friends and family in and outside of the church, could be one of sharing of stories about lost sons and fathers—stories where, despite the hard eclipses of life, God is always with us, and still calls us. I wish that my life was less full of hiding and more full of responses like the one spoken by a grown-up Karen in the final line of "Tongues of Fire": "Here I am, Lord."

{ 2 }

Walking with a Limp

I was in the local grocery store the other night, trying to move through it in a relatively efficient manner, when I noticed something I have encountered more often lately. As I pulled my cart into aisle two, a man was talking to the cereal boxes. Now, earlier in my lifetime, my peers and I would associate this behavior with a certain mental illness. When I was in college and would visit my sister in Los Angeles, we would meet up with people such as this with some regularity. I remember one tall, intimidating sort of woman who was wearing a heavy raincoat on an eighty-degree day, lumbering down Hollywood Boulevard. She took a particular interest in me as we passed, pointing at me and shouting, "I know who you are!" (She never told me, though, and the lack of identification has haunted me for years.) However, as I passed the man in aisle two, who by now was having a heated conversation with a box of muesli, I realized that we no longer so identify people such as this man.

Instead, we call them people who constantly talk on cell phones while they wear headsets.

I confess that I still do not accept this as normal behavior. People who do these things tend to also drive their cars and swerve, or sit next to a perfectly fine person on a bus but insist on conversing with someone who is not present. They walk down the street alone, talking and gesturing. Sometimes I want to pull their cars over and ask them to concentrate on their driving before they hurt themselves or someone else. I want them to speak more discreetly so that I am not privy to their personal matters.

This problem has come to mind of late for a few reasons: I lost my cell phone, and the replacement came packaged with a headset, so I am having a personal crisis in wondering what to do with it; I am becoming a much less patient driver and find that my tolerance is waning for the mixture of poor driving and cell phones; and all of this reminded me of a period, a few years ago, before we moved from the Midwest to the West Coast, when I was having trouble with church.

Our pastor had experienced an illness over the course of a year during which the pace of the church itself seemed to be thrown off. We would never know what would happen from week to week. Second, we had a new Sunday school teacher—a *young* man who looked like he probably used a headset for his cell phone when he drove, someone who liked to start adult Sunday school with icebreakers, someone who was a good teacher. We also had a number of new people attending—mainly young people—but really a number of people from all sorts of age groups, backgrounds, and cultures. Now, although this is a warm church, it is still a church populated by parents, their children, their grandchildren, and even memories of those parents' parents—that is to say, if you're an outsider, it takes a while to get your name on the church birthday list for the monthly newsletter. And even though

I knew that the church's welcome could be more hesitant than it should be in some cases for these newcomers, I found myself personally being just as hesitant. This realization, combined with my lack of warmth for the new, gifted Sunday school teacher, bothered me deeply.

I often use Jesus's parable of the prodigal son in my introduction to literature courses to explain the structure of fiction, and the problem of point of view. Depending on whom one takes as the story's main character—the younger, rebellious son who is welcomed home after his exploits, or the older brother who stays home and seems to get little reward for his good behavior—one can understand the story in significantly different ways. In his book on postmodernism and the church, *The End of the World . . . As We Know It,* pastor Chuck Smith Jr., uses the parable of the prodigal son to discuss the cultural gap facing a generation of people who, once being the newcomers in congregations, now find themselves as part of the old guard, part of the church establishment. Oftentimes we haven't even noticed this was happening—we were busy raising small children who suddenly became teenagers, we became young people trapped in bodies that gained weight, lost hair, and developed crow's feet at the corners of our eyes. Smith writes,

> Churches must re-examine the way they respond to Generation X and how much allowance they will give this generation to develop . . . its own ways of practicing the faith. Will our churches host the party for Xers who want to return to the Father? The problem, staying to the story of the prodigal, is that most of our churches are not under the administration of the father, but of the older brother. (65)

This sort of comment is uncomfortable and, annoyingly, correct. What has happened to the older brother in the parable is not just generational; it can happen to any believer. Despite his complaint of personal responsibility, and his accusation that his younger brother is just an ungrateful slacker, despite all the issues related to turf and insiders and outsiders, the problem with the older brother is his heart. "Look," he cries to his father over his brother's return, "all these years I've been slaving for you and never disobeying your orders!" When did the older brother start thinking of himself as a slave? When did he begin to become annoyed with the likes of people who drove and talked on cell phones at the same time? When did he begin to be uncomfortable around people who obviously didn't know how they were expected to behave and think in church? When did he become jealous of gifted, energetic, younger people? When, really, did he start thinking of himself as an indentured worker, and stop thinking of himself as his father's son?

I also remember some of the other older brothers and sisters of my own "Christian youth." Shortly after my conversion, two of them asked me, outside of church one evening, if I was a Christian. I thought this was an odd topic to share with total strangers. I said yes, but what was I to do in return—ask them the same? Was this some sort of Christian code? They weren't interested in conversation, however; they were interested in my cigarette. Why, they wondered, if I was a Christian, was I smoking? I was too floored to respond. Perhaps there were more important things in life to be concerned about. Perhaps, I should have said, if you're having trouble with my cigarette, then I don't think you're ready to hear about my other issues.

But there were other, better examples of older brothers and sisters. During that same period of time I spent many evenings at a local pancake restaurant that was known to be owned and operated by Christians. My pre-Christian road indeed had been hard and ridiculously messy, and I'm sure I looked worse for the wear. I spent most of my time there reading my Bible, drinking in the words and an occasional cup of coffee, occupying a table, not doing much for business. And yet I remember the older brothers and sisters there—the waitresses and the owner who would always greet me as if I were the host of a paying party of ten, who would refill my coffee, and smile at me, and probably pray for me. And remembering their example, I know how, many years later, I should now be acting toward my younger siblings—and all of my brothers and sisters—in Christ.

My Almost Experience with Anne Lamott

A few years ago, the midwestern Christian university at which I was employed invited author Anne Lamott to campus. Such invitations are not given or accepted lightly. Lamott is an extremely successful writer, and thus a rather pricey speaker. Moreover, she is controversial in some circles—she takes strong political stances not usually associated with evangelical Christianity, and writes about subjects and in language that make many people, particularly many Christians, uncomfortable. Her life, before and after her conversion, does not fit the stereotypical life of the Christian convert. Thus, her reception in such circles is unpredictable, and I imagine that she may experience anxiety about accepting speaking engagements at such places. I have long been a fan of Lamott—I have taught a collection of her essays on faith, *Traveling Mercies,* in first-year writing courses, and had recommended that we incorporate the book into a humanities course required of all first-year students, a course that dealt with some of life's great questions. As luck would have it, I was out of the country when Lamott spoke, so I can only relay the reaction to her lecture secondhand.

From all accounts, she was sharp, funny, direct, and not at all afraid of questions—not surprising if you have read any of her books. The surprise was more about who attended the lecture. The university received phone calls before and after the event thanking us for bringing Lamott to campus and telling stories of how much her writing had meant to them. Now, the university has been in the same location for over a hundred years and yet, before Anne Lamott's lecture, was unknown to many of the callers. What about Lamott, as opposed to other capable speakers who come to campus, attracted this audience?

In an interesting juxtaposition to this phenomenon was the reaction of students at our university to Lamott. When I had taught *Traveling Mercies* three years before as part of a first-year writing course, a number of the students there had extremely positive reactions that were similar to those expressed by the visitors at her lecture. Additionally, there was an appreciation of Lamott's skill as an author: her ability to personalize difficult questions, to be candid and vulnerable with strangers over issues of struggle and faith, and the simple beauty of her prose. However, when *Traveling Mercies* moved into the new, required first-year course, the reaction changed. For most students, a course that claims to bring participants into dialogue with life's great questions has unquestionably high stakes, and the word *required* can evoke suspicion and some hostility. The expectations move beyond those of "simply" education and instead become those we might associate more with a church experience: we expect models of living, we are on the lookout for doctrinal distress; in short, we have high expectations because we know how important the conversation is, and how influential gifted writers and speakers can be.

The reaction of my section of mainly eighteen-year-olds was fascinating: Lamott was too liberal, perhaps Lamott was not really a Christian, one cannot claim Christianity and engage in the sort of behavior in which Lamott engages, how could one be a Christian and hold such political positions. Voilà! We were in the parable of the prodigal son—we had a room full of eighteen-year-old older sisters and brothers. I am not discounting the validity of the questions, and I understand that these students are experiencing a particular stage of development, as they move from accepting external authority to internalizing that authority—a stage in which questioning black-and-white ways of looking at the world can be seen as a threat. Instead, I am questioning their memories. About two-thirds of the way through a particularly acrimonious discussion of *Traveling Mercies,* during which a number of students were wondering how Lamott can claim Christian conversion and still engage in the behavior that she describes, the conversation was stopped dead in its tracks. A student who had not been afraid to speak up during the rest of the course had been peculiarly quiet during the Lamott discussions. During this class meeting, I thought I could see her agitation growing. Finally, she interrupted the discussion, saying, "But that's how I was. Before I became a Christian, that's how I was. And sometimes I'm still like that."

I would argue that the positive public reaction to Anne Lamott's lecture at our university was both heartfelt and unfortunately unusual in Christian circles because Lamott is able to speak to those people who have recently found God, or who are still on the outside. Lamott speaks as a younger sibling instead of an older one. The uncomfortable implication, of course, concerns how we who are inside various Christian institutions speak, or perhaps do not speak, to them.

Correct Behavior and the Problem of Patriarchs

One of the blessings that my transplanted family experienced during our years in the Midwest was a yearly trip to visit friends and family back "home" in California. On one occasion I spent a few December mornings writing outside in the front courtyard of the house of some friends. These friends knew the highlights and the darker moments of our premarried lives—the husband and I were best men at each other's weddings and roommates during what our youngest children like to refer to as our "sad" bachelor days; we all have seen each other through the shining moments and self-doubts of careers, parenthood, our weaknesses, life's unforeseen disasters, and simply that continuing journey of maturation. During our stay with them I was working on updating a sermon I would give after vacation at my university's chapel. Our chaplain had offered us speakers a challenge: take a story from the Bible and live it, be creative, speak in the voice of one of the characters. I decided to write from the point of view of the Old Testament patriarch Jacob, someone whose life wasn't exactly exemplary, and who knew very well the kind of person he was, but someone whom God chose anyway. I updated Jacob's story so that it took place in southern California in contemporary times. And so when one of our friends one evening picked up my handwritten manuscript, began to read, and asked me if this was an "autobiographical piece," I wanted to both laugh and cry. I wondered how far she had read in the story.

Jacob is a spiritual conundrum. He is listed in Hebrews as one of the heroes of the faith, and yet he is a person about whom I have heard some of the nastiest things said—from pulpits—during the course of my Christian life. Jacob is a cheat. Jacob is a liar. Jacob is an example of someone who calls himself faithful, but who never really enters into a saving relationship with God.

The latter, I think, is the lowest blow one professing Christian can level at another.

I ended up delivering the sermon during the time when *Traveling Mercies* was first making its controversial sweep through the Christian community, as it sold well amidst a broader national audience. I first heard of Lamott during that winter via another chapel sermon—this one by our university's president, who spoke about Lamott's description of her life of faith and the negative reactions he had heard in the Christian community. If you press these readers, they admit that what makes them most uncomfortable with Lamott's life—similar to their discomfort with Jacob—is that her encounters with God and, most especially, her life experiences before *and* after that encounter, are too problematic. They are afraid that someone would read *Traveling Mercies* and get the wrong idea about what it means to become a Christian.

Jacob's life is consistent with a number of the patriarchs'—but with fewer positive points. Hebrews 11 cites his act of faith—the action that serves as proof of his faith and his credentials for being listed with the others in Hebrews 11—in terms of his life's end:

> By faith Jacob, when he was dying, blessed each of Joseph's sons, and worshiped as he leaned on the top of his staff. (Heb. 11:21)

This doesn't sound like much, but, as we will see, the act of faith is significant given the context of Jacob's life.

Here is a short summation of the biblical account of Jacob's life. (If he is an insignificant character in the Bible, or one whom we should reject rather than one from whom we should learn, then why does God spend parts of twenty-three chapters in Genesis on his life?) He is the younger twin brother of Esau, the son of

Isaac and grandchild of Abraham. The negatives of his life are plenteous, even from the very beginning. As the children emerge from Rebekah's womb, Jacob grabs at Esau's heel, seeming to want his brother's position as firstborn, but also in an indication of the desperation in which he will live his life. Jacob always, it seems, grasps at what he cannot easily have. His name itself is not flattering: figuratively, it means "he who deceives." Despite the assurance given to his mother by God that Jacob and his descendants will actually be served by Esau and his children, Jacob's early life is full of deceit in striving to gain what God has already promised—and he leaves casualties in his wake. Jacob bargains a hungry Esau out of his birthright. Then, through a stealth action planned by his mother, he gains his almost-blind father's coveted blessing by disguising himself as his older brother. To escape Esau's wrath, he flees to the house of his uncle Laban, where he seems to meet his match in deceit. Jacob is tricked into working for Laban for fourteen years in exchange for his two daughters—the elder of whom he never wanted, but who is given to him first. His wages are changed by his uncle ten times over twenty total years of servitude in order to benefit his employer. In attempting to please his second wife, Jacob sleeps with concubines to produce children for the barren Rachel, only to complicate his family situation further. Rather than confront his wife, he leaves Laban's house in secret, an act which jeopardizes him further through Rachel's thievery. He attempts to bribe Esau upon his return, fearing his older brother's grudge and temper.

Jacob constantly bargains with God, and moreover, despite God's faithfulness, he seems ever hesitant to fulfill his end of the bargain. Jacob seems to have little control over his own children: among them are a murderer and a rapist, and his youngest child, Joseph, seems ready to follow in his father's footsteps, taunting his older brothers mercilessly, telling them that he will rule over them, until one day they sell him into slavery and convince Jacob that his favorite has been killed by wild beasts. Joseph lives apart from Jacob in Egypt, all the time assumed dead by his father. When reunited with his son at last, he weeps a life's worth of tears. In the forty-seventh chapter of Genesis, after being reunited with Joseph, Jacob is brought before Pharaoh. By merit of his old age, he is a bit of a curiosity by then. Joseph leads him into the presence of the leader of the known world, and *Jacob* blesses *him*. Pharaoh, doubtless amused, then asks Jacob how old he is:

> And Jacob said to Pharaoh, "The years of my pilgrimage are a hundred and thirty. My years have been few and difficult, and they do not equal the years of the pilgrimage of my fathers." (Gen. 47:9)

This is certainly a cautionary note. Who of us wants to come to the end of his or her years and feel that the numbers of days we have been given have not been enough, and that our journeys have been fraught with failures? And this man, followed by troubles of his own making, is a hero of the faith?

The act of faith of which Hebrew 11 speaks is recorded in Genesis 48, as Jacob's health begins to fail in his old age:

> Jacob said to Joseph, "God Almighty appeared to me at Luz in the land of Canaan, and there he blessed me and said to me, 'I am going to make you fruitful and will increase your numbers. I will make you a community of peoples, and I will give this land as an everlasting possession to your descendants after you.'
>
> "Now then, your two sons born to you in Egypt will be reckoned as mine. . . ."
>
> Israel said to Joseph, "I never expected to see your face again, and now God has allowed me to see your children too."

Then Joseph removed [the two children] from his knees and bowed down with his face to the ground. And Jacob took both of them, Ephraim on his right . . . and Manasseh on his left . . . and brought them close to him. . . .

Then he blessed Joseph and said, "May the God before whom my fathers Abraham and Isaac walked, the God who has been my Shepherd all my life to this day, the Angel who has delivered me from all harm—may he bless these boys. May they be called by my name and the names of my fathers Abraham and Isaac, and may they increase greatly upon the earth."

When Joseph saw his father placing his right hand on Ephraim's head [the head of the younger child] he was displeased . . . [and] said to him, "No, my father, this one is the firstborn; put your right hand on his head."

But his father refused and said, "I know, my son, I know. . . . Nevertheless, his younger brother will be greater than he. . . ." (Gen. 48:3–19)

Despite the overwhelming failure of his life, Jacob is able in confidence to give God's blessing to his grandchildren, and in doing so offers a blessing that will go against all social convention and the wishes of his favorite son. Despite his less-than-exemplary life, he calls God his shepherd and deliverer. How can we ignore God's intervention and question the status of Jacob's faith? Perhaps the conversation of the older brother and the father in Jesus's parable is applicable here as well:

The older brother became angry and refused to go in [to the party welcoming his younger brother home]. So his father went out and pleaded with him. But he answered his father, "Look! All these years I've been slaving for you and never disobeyed your orders. Yet you never gave me even a young goat so I could celebrate with my friends. But when this son of yours who has squandered your property with prostitutes comes home, you kill the fattened calf for him!"

"My son," the father said, "you are always with me, and everything I have is yours. But we had to celebrate and be glad, because this brother of yours was dead and is alive again; he was lost and is found." (Luke 15:28–32)

A few years ago, I experienced Christian reactions to Jacob again, this time in an adult Sunday school class. The only word fitting enough to describe the reaction of almost everyone in the class is *visceral*. People who are usually the nicest folks you would ever want to meet, people who do not appear to have lost their tempers in the last decade, react to Jacob with something akin to someone troubled by a familial scar. He is like that one person in the family, or that one thing a certain person did so many years ago, that you, like the older brother in the parable, have never been able to dig out from under your own skin. It is one thing to talk about family relations, another to live them. And, perhaps, it is one thing to talk about original sin, and another to honestly see the effects of it. I think that Jacob touches some sort of familial nerve that encourages us to establish our distance from him, because it speaks to us so much of ourselves. We question whether he was ever "saved" at all.

> It is one thing to talk about family relations, another to live them.

Jacob, in his spiritual life, walks with a limp. I'm referring, of course, to his encounter with the angel as described in Genesis 32, the night before he is to face his brother Esau again. He encounters the angel of the Lord and wrestles with him, hanging on for dear life until he gets the angel to agree to bless him. It is during this moment that God changes his name from "deceiver" to "he has struggled with God and men and has overcome." The angel touches Jacob's hip during this process, and the resulting limp that will be with him for the rest of his days is symbolic as well. It reminds Jacob of all of the untidy struggles and sins of his life: his unredeemed actions, mind-sets, decisions. These are all painful to remember, but the limp reminds him both of the sin and of the fact that he overcame. To live with such a limp is uncomfortable for us as Christians—I often desire to be quite conscious of the fact that Jesus's death saves us from our sin, but I am much less eager to remember the sins we have been saved from. I don't like being reminded of these sins when I see them in others. Perhaps this is what bothers each of us in such a visceral way about Jacob. It is one thing to study Jacob in Sunday school, separated by the safety of millennia. It is another thing to encounter the realities of Jacob's life in the present day, in our very own lives and in the foibles from which we have been—and are being—redeemed and transformed. That would be a dangerous conversation, and whoever begins it might not expect a lot of thanks. And for this, we return to Anne Lamott.

An Account of a Journey

Traveling Mercies is a cleverly disguised spiritual autobiography. The very title tells us this, in that it points to an account of a journey—a process of going from a very human place of sin and failure into an encounter with God. And when one encounters God, the journey and the transformation do not stop. Upon meeting God, life becomes a journey, understood in light of the life-changing encounter, filled with faith in a new direction and an ultimate purpose and mercy. It is an account of love expressed from God to the believer, and from the believer to others. Spiritual autobiography is a genre that produces bridges—it confesses the before, the after, and the continuing of one's life with God.

Probably the most famous spiritual autobiography is Augustine's *Confessions*, a book that is still required reading at some point in the undergraduate careers of many college students. *Confessions* was written at the end of the fourth century in North Africa by a Christian bishop, and it is Augustine's reflection from middle age on the sins of youth and a journey to God. Augustine reflects on his sexual appetites as a young man, his intellectual struggles with the notions of who God is and how life should be lived, his experiences of friendship (both healthy and unhealthy), and a common-law marriage that produced for him a son. He spends a significant amount of time on an act of theft in his youth—stealing pears from a neighbor's tree—that in his mind epitomizes much of what was wrong with his soul. Augustine's road to God is a slow one, and its course is not apparent when he is traveling it. Nonetheless, most of the story is told from the point of view of becoming a Christian, and in retrospect Augustine's path to God becomes clear.

Anne Lamott's *Traveling Mercies* is Augustine's *Confessions* as it could be written in the late twentieth or early twenty-first century, with all of the markers that show our culture's recent history and present interests: a baby boomer of the sixties drug culture coming of age; a woman narrating the autobiography instead of a man; a lack of philosophical clarity of what it means to journey from spiritual (and almost physical) death to life; an emphasis on experience and self over theology and God. That is, Lamott's book reflects our time's ways of thinking in the same way that Augustine's reflected his. It is hard for students—particularly those outside of the Christian faith tradition—to read and appreciate Augustine, precisely because his culture and his very way of thinking have become foreign to us. But in his own time, just as Lamott does now, Augustine spoke to the concerns of the day.

Critics of Anne Lamott's story on these levels—those who prefer the clean-cut theology of Augustine or the chronologically removed safety of Jacob, and who perhaps hope for a more Augustinian and evidently orthodox coming to faith than what Lamott (and Jacob's story) offers—perhaps have lost sight of the reality that both Augustine's autobiography and Jacob's story spoke to their audiences from a position of vulnerability. Regarding Augustine, members of twenty-first-century culture might wonder what all the fuss is over stealing pears from a neighbor's tree, or, regarding Jacob, over the stealing of a birthright. These same readers, however, know very much, either directly or vicariously, about the depths of alcoholism and eating disorders, family dysfunction, sexual tension, death and loss and the fear of both, and the anxieties of declaring a faith that makes no sense to one's closest friends. For a moment, think of the dilemma of modern faith as two people standing on different sides of a gorge. On one side is a member of our culture, and the landscape on that side is the culture itself. On the other side is a Christian and the landscape of his or her subculture. The Christian and the landscape certainly look foreign, in ways intriguing, frightening, and even unattractive to the member of culture. And yet it often seems that the best the Christian can do for his neighbor in terms of an invitation to come to the other side is to simply yell, "Jump!" There isn't enough motivation. The neighbor might want to come closer, but there is not a bridge upon which he or she may cross the divide. Thus, enter the bridge: enter Jacob, enter Anne Lamott.

Lamott writes,

My coming to faith did not start with a leap but rather a series of staggers from what seemed like one safe place to another. Like lily pads, round and green, these places summoned and then held me up while I grew. . . .Yet each step brought me closer to the verdant pad of faith on which I somehow stay afloat today. (*Traveling Mercies*, 3)

If we or our neighbors ever wonder aloud concerning the Bible's relevance to our lives today, we might want to consider juxtaposing parallel lives separated by 3,000 or so years. Jacob, Anne Lamott, and we ourselves can enter into a conversation about the deep inherent difficulties of life, the road to God, finding him, and still walking with a limp. Our personal limps serve as evidence of our difficulties and remind us of our need for him, the truth about ourselves, and the futility of trying to keep up appearances. Lamott tells difficult truths about conversion: its path sometimes is evident only in retrospect; the water on which the lily pads rest is deep and dangerous; the safe places aren't what we expect but always what we need; and it is hard to understand the depth of a convert's change without looking at the depths from which he or she (and all of us—younger and older siblings alike) come. *Traveling Mercies* takes its reader through stages similar to those found in God's story of Jacob's life and probably in our own stories.

Naming, Renaming, and Slow Transformation

As we discovered before, Jacob's given name actually implied a dishonest child: "heel-catcher," "deceiver." The words spoken by parents over their children were powerful in Jacob's culture. When Jacob steals his brother's blessing, living up to his name in deceiving his father, Isaac, the old man pronounces the following:

> May God give you of heaven's dew
> And of earth's richness—

An abundance of grain and new wine.
May nations serve you
and peoples bow down to you. . . .
May those who curse you be cursed
And those who bless you be blessed. (Gen. 27:28–29)

Such blessings were considered finite. When Esau comes too late to claim the blessing that his brother has already taken, Isaac can only offer:

Your dwelling will be
away from earth's richness,
away from the dew of heaven above.
You will live by the sword
and you will serve your brother.
But when you grow restless,
You will throw his yoke
From off your neck. (Gen. 27:39–40)

Our society—though of course in seemingly less supernatural ways—believes in the power of names as well: we apply them to each other early and often. Lamott grew up in what by almost anyone's measure would have been a politically and philosophically progressive family, yet where the old human behavior of naming still applies.

All my life men had been nudging my dad and saying there must have been a nigger in the woodpile, I guess because of both [my] hair and my big heavy-lidded eyes. And my father, who never once in his life would have used the word nigger, would smile and give an almost imperceptible laugh—not a trace of rage on behalf of black people, not a trace of rage on behalf of me. (*Traveling Mercies*, 12)

So I was doing well academically, and I was a well-ranked tennis player and was the apple of my father's eye—and then I would bring home a report card with a B-plus on it, and my parents would look at the report card as if I'd flunked. "Uh, honey?" one of them would ask, looking perplexed. "Now, this isn't a criticism but, if you could get a B-plus in philosophy, how much harder would it have been to get an A-minus?" (19)

The results, unfortunately, are predictable. They are results I have seen in the lives of too many of the students I have taught in college.

Drugs helped. More than anything else, they gave me the feeling that I was fine and life was good and something sacred shimmered on its edges.

Being sexual with boys helped, too. . . . Being loved by my teachers helped, but then report cards would come out, and once again I would think I had fallen short. (20)

Both Lamott and Jacob are renamed by God, but the traces of the old names take a long time to dispel and continue to affect behavior: *cheat, deceiver, not one of us, inadequate.* Jacob struggles with his prior names. In times of trouble we see him falling back both on God and on what worked before—his own skill at padding the odds. He prays *and* deceives when he is confronted with an uncle who changes his wages and holds him captive; he prays *and* tries to placate when he meets his brother after the passing of so many years. The difference is that *he prays at all,* that he is in relationship, and the difference is day and night. Lamott's behavior may be troubling to Christian readers who insist on a fast, antiseptic change. Like Jacob, she falls back on the behavior that "helped" before in her darkest hours, but she both prays and reverts. And, gradually, she changes.

Lamott has been "named" in another way: she is the daughter of an alcoholic. She learned this behavior as a method of dealing with crisis, and she inherited the physiological markers that make her vulnerable to alcohol and to addiction generally. Thus, in her life, before she had turned thirty, her family had fallen apart, she herself had become an alcoholic, she had an eating disorder, and she had a number of other addictions as well. She was poor. She seemed incapable of establishing healthy relationships with men. As Lamott herself stated,

> I was cracking up. It was like a cartoon where something gets hit, and one crack appears, which spider webs outward until the whole pane or vase cracks and hangs suspended for a moment before falling into a pile of powder on the floor. . . .
>
> Then one afternoon in my dark bedroom, the cracks webbed all the way through me. I believed that I would die soon, from a fall or an overdose. I knew there was an afterlife but felt that the odds of my living long enough to get into heaven were almost nil. They couldn't possibly take you in the shape I was in. I could no longer imagine how God loved me. (*Traveling Mercies*, 39–42)

When Lamott is at the very end of her rope, a conversation and ensuing friendship with an Anglican priest and regular visits to a small Presbyterian church (to hear the singing) begin to turn the path of her life. But then, after another failed relationship, an abortion, and the physical complications that followed, she is at the edge of death, alone in her room, drunk and bleeding.

> Several hours later, the blood stopped flowing, and I got in bed, shaky and sad and too wild to have another drink or take a sleeping pill. I had a cigarette and turned off the light. After a while, as I lay there, I became aware of someone with me, hunkered down in the corner. . . . The feeling was so strong that I actually turned

on the light for a moment to make sure no one was there—of course, there wasn't. But after a while, in the dark again, I knew beyond any doubt that it was Jesus. I felt him as surely as I feel my dog lying nearby as I write this.

And I was appalled. I thought about my life and my brilliant hilarious progressive friends, I thought about what everyone would think of me if I became a Christian, and it seemed an utterly impossible thing that simply could not be allowed to happen. I turned to the wall and said out loud, "I would rather die."

I felt him just sitting there on his haunches in the corner of my sleeping loft, watching me with patience and love. . . . (49)

One week later, after never losing the sense that this presence was following her around in her daily life, she stays for the sermon in the Presbyterian church, which she "thought was so ridiculous, like someone trying to convince me of the existence of extraterrestrials" (50). The music washes over her, and she has the sense of "something" rocking her in its bosom, but she flees the church. Arriving home, the presence still there, she declares to Jesus that she gives up. For the more sensitive reader, I have avoided her less palatable language:

I took a long deep breath and said out loud, "All right. You can come in."

So this was my beautiful moment of conversion. (50)

To become and stay sober after her conversion (three years at the time of writing *Traveling Mercies*) and be able to understand that she will always be an addict is a behavioral change that very few people are capable of making. To lose her father to malignant melanoma and then to learn to trust God during a biopsy on one of her own moles is heroic; Lamott treats it as an opportunity, mostly, for self-deprecating humor. An example of gradual change in *Traveling Mercies* that likely troubles us older siblings is her sexual behavior after her conversion. She continues to seek relationships with men and continues to have sex with men. What she seeks in those relationships begins to change, however, and when she becomes pregnant by a man who has no interest whatsoever in being a father, she keeps the baby after putting the decision in God's hands through prayer. We start at different places before our conversions. For some of us, the "limp" we carry into our Christian life isn't so readily noticeable, or we have become experts at hiding it. For others, the limp is too obvious, and we are tired of putting on spiritual camouflage.

The Christian Life as Mercies in Our Travels

Lamott's spiritual autobiography consists first of a generally chronological narrative, which I just described, named "Lily Pads," in which she describes her condition before and at the time of her conversion. The book afterward is divided into smaller chapters, some of which found their genesis as stand-alone articles. While the easy tone of Lamott's writing may encourage the reader to see these merely as "some thoughts on faith," the chapters focus on particular aspects of the Christian life that encourage and allow her to *keep living* the Christian life. These aspects mainly center on the troubles and lurches of faith that accompany growth, and the necessity of welcoming places to come home to.

In talking about the portion of her life in which she was coming to faith, Lamott relates an episode in college when she learns of Kierkegaard and his retelling of the story of Abraham and Isaac. Lamott describes Abraham's faith in spite of evidence, his decision to consider God loving and trustworthy despite what Abraham is initially asked to do. She writes that she left class that day feeling "changed, and a little crazy," still like a badly damaged, unassembled jigsaw puzzle, but one that now "at least [had] a few border pieces in place." Lamott returns to this metaphor often in describing the Christian life after conversion, suggesting that this sort of interaction with God does not end with the one-time decision but continues as an expected part of a relationship with God, in which the divine enters our world to stretch our spirits and to comfort us.

> For some of us, the "limp" we carry into our Christian life isn't so readily noticeable, or we have become experts at hiding it. For others, the limp is too obvious, and we are tired of putting on spiritual camouflage.

She writes in the chapter entitled "Traveling Mercies" of an incident with a newly purchased used car that decides to break down, in pouring rain, while she and her son are trying to get to the bedside of a terminally ill friend. The incident of the car becomes a metaphor for how the whole world seems at times: broken, and continuing in a process of breaking that seems to thwart our best attempts at practicing love and finding plot and meaning. Yet the story is also about the small miracles that surround such moments of darkness, and the way God has of turning the worst brokenness the world can offer into moments that are glued back in unexpected ways. The seemingly unacceptable delay allows Lamott to be with her friend days later instead, to comfort her at the time of her death. In "The Mole," Lamott walks us through our fears of death—for her, that she would follow her father's path through cancer and leave her young son orphaned—and allows us to see that God can break such circles and give us fellowship in which we can find confession and comfort.

But the most important lesson about the postconversion life in *Traveling Mercies* seems to me to be about Christian community—to put it ungracefully, a community of limpers. We are not talking about Christianity as a crutch for avoiding our problems; we instead are talking about Christian community as a place where problems are honestly confessed and help is gained. In these communities, people who have lost their notion of "plot" for their lives struggle to discern and accept God's plot, God's story. In one metaphor of her chapter "Barn Raising," Lamott talks of a neighbor child, Olivia, who is given a diagnosis of cystic fibrosis, and of the chaos that follows in her family. But Lamott's community is there, "walking the dog, taking the kids to the park, cleaning the kitchen, and letting Sara and Adam [Olivia's parents] hate what was going on when they needed to." But in doing this, in embracing both the reality of the catastrophe and the family that has experienced it, Lamott claims that her community is building a house, raising a barn together when the strength of one family alone simply will not do: "We, their friends, all know the rains and the wind will come, and they will be cold—oh, God, they will be cold. But then we will come too, I said; we will have been building this barn all along, and so there will always be shelter" (154–55).

Lamott's episodes of wrestling *within* the Christian community are some of the most honest I have read. In "Forgiveness," she describes one in a series of Christian counterparts with whom she is prone to trouble. Lamott is a single mother, politically liberal, and vocationally unorthodox—there are, of course, real tensions that go with such a modus operandi. She is having particular trouble with the mother of one of her son Sam's friends. This mother is conservative, traditional, and rather competent in her job description as a mother. She tries to reach out to Lamott, but the differences in culture do not fare well in the encounters.

At one point, after having read one of Lamott's earlier books, a journal of her son's first year called *Operating Instructions,* the woman confides to Lamott that maybe it's a good thing Lamott's kindergarten-aged son is having trouble reading. Lamott comes to the conclusion, however, that she herself, not the woman, is the problem. And from this realization community begins to form.

In "Knocking on Heaven's Door," she is on an airplane during an episode of extreme turbulence (both spiritual and physical) involving a storm, a heart attack, and a conservative Christian man who is singing the praises of the *Left Behind* series to her. As the crises resolve, the differences, for the moment at least, melt away.

It is in this particular essay, though, that Lamott also introduces her tour de force on Christian community, through the description of her own church. Lamott tells us that Ken, who has advanced AIDS, has begun to attend her church. His partner dies, and, says Lamott, "A few weeks later Ken told us that . . . Jesus had slid into the hole in his heart that Brandon's loss left, and had been there ever since. . . . He says now that he would gladly pay any price for what he has now, which is Jesus, and us" (64). One of the women in the church is not comfortable with who Ken is and where he has been, and is uncertain of how to deal with him. Until one morning, after which the congregation has sung, interestingly enough, "Jacob's Ladder," the woman picks Ken up into her arms during the fellowship hymn, "His Eye Is on the Sparrow":

And Ranola . . . went to his side and bent down to lift him up— lifted up this white rag doll, this scarecrow. She held him next to her, draped over and against her like a child while they sang. And it pierced me. (65)

It is the nature of the human being, and especially those human beings who have encountered Jesus, to walk through life limping. At one point in *Operating Instructions*, Lamott is having regrets about not being a perfect mother, not having a husband, and worrying about how this will affect her son's welcome into the world. She is reminded of "five rules of the world" as outlined by a Tom Weston, a Catholic priest:

> The first rule . . . is that you must not have anything wrong with you or anything different. The second one is that if you do have something wrong with you, you must get over it as soon as possible. The third rule is that if you can't get over it, you must pretend that you have. The fourth rule is that if you can't pretend you have, you shouldn't show up. You should stay home, because it's hard for everyone else to have you around. And the fifth rule is that if you are going to insist on showing up, you should at least have the decency to feel ashamed. (*Operating Instructions*, 100)

So, Christian biography and autobiography is a countercultural activity. God holds little back in writing down the lives of the patriarchs. Augustine and Lamott and other Christian autobiographers hold little back in their confessions. That's the nature of the community: we are confessional. By entering, we have already admitted that the perfect people are all outside. To pretend otherwise only means that it is probably time to check our memories.

{ 3 }

Darkness: Does My Life Have a Plot?

I am doomed to remember a boy with a wrecked voice . . . because he is the reason I believe in God; I am a Christian because of Owen Meany. (1)

—John Irving, *A Prayer for Owen Meany*

My second son, Eric, had colic. Those parents who have experienced this condition need to hear no more. The infants who experience it are miserable, lucky only in the sense that they are too little to remember it later. I myself remember only patches of that period of my life, because of the sleep deprivation that resulted from my son's inability to settle and sleep.

Here was our routine: my wife would put him down at about 9:00 or 9:30 by walking him around and around the bedroom, lights off, until he became tired, or perhaps dizzy—who knows which? He would then sleep for two hours until, awoken by the pain in his abdomen, it was my shift. I would then walk him around the room until his sleep or dizziness returned. But about once a week, this did not settle him back down, so I would take him for a ride in our car through the long, open, deserted streets of our suburb at 1:00 in the morning or so, until the hum of the engine and the vibration of the road would put him out for the night. I am one of those people who believe that God helps us greatly when we have very little, even in small ways. Back then, when both my wife and I were in school and our wallets were usually empty, God helped us a lot. Our car had no business running as well as it did. And in our suburb, the local police had a reputation for pulling over people who they didn't think belonged in town—people who drove well-worn cars like ours, or who were not young, or who were not white. My fear was that at 1:00 in the morning, my son and I would be pulled over and he would awaken and would never go back to sleep. But in the year of his colic we were never pulled over, and the old car hummed along like magic under the moonlight.

One night the colic was bad enough that neither the endless pacing nor even the driving worked. Terry and I became desperate, until finally, in my delirium, it occurred to me that the answer was alcohol! Just this one time, we would give Eric a small shot, and he would be asleep in no time. We are not really drinkers, and all we could find in the house was a bottle of cooking sherry. Nonetheless, we reasoned, a potion is a potion. Terry reluctantly agreed to hold the baby while I took a dropperful of sherry, opened Eric's mouth, and shot the liquid directly at the back of his throat.

His eyes widened at the shock of the alcohol's burn. Then he grew silent and seemed to calm a little. Terry walked him around the room. I turned down the light. We smiled at each other: we were geniuses! Eric melted onto his mother's shoulder, and as I made my way for the door, he began to sing. It was soft at first, and not very melodious. Then he raised his head, waved it back and forth a little, and began to sing a little louder. This went on, I think, for hours. We were exhausted, and our experiment had only taught us that our year-old son was a happy drunk.

The colic abated at about fourteen months, but something else began to materialize. Eric seemed distracted—a bit like teenagers are distracted almost all of the time: a little sullen, not entirely present, a bit withdrawn. Photographs we have of him during that time show him seeming to look through the camera to something unseen. His affect was often flat—but not always so. At times he was right there with you; at others, he seemed almost limp, as if he were making a supreme effort to just keep himself vertical. (A picture we have kept from that time is actually one in a series of proofs. Terry had taken Eric and our eldest son to a local photo shop to surprise me with portraits. In the meltdown that ensued in front of the camera, unfortunately the only surprise that took place was the amount of time it took Terry to recover from the ordeal.) Eric's walking and speech were a little delayed—but the same had been true with our first son. Yet, he did not raise his hands to us when we picked him up from child care.

And then life became busier.

As I was about to complete graduate school, we experienced a strong sense of God's call to move out of southern California in order to accept a job in Chicago—this was one of those rare moments when the sense of calling was so strong that I felt God's voice was almost audible, and the sense of his presence was almost physically palpable. And Terry became pregnant with our third child, due a month and a half after our scheduled move. So we raced through the ensuing months: a dissertation to complete, housing to find 2,000 miles away, graduation, and the final picture: a family without many monetary resources, a wife eight months pregnant, loading up the moving van and moving to the Midwest—my ancestral home, but a place where Terry and I had never lived.

Eric showed signs of stress over the move—as he had always demonstrated in new situations—but the scenario worsened as the summer turned to fall. We found ourselves carefully planning our daily schedule, carefully timing trips to the grocery store or the mall so that Eric would not become tired or hungry. When these trips were not well planned, we found ourselves in the middle of two- or three-hour inconsolable meltdowns, where Eric would simply go into overload in the middle of a public area. At home, his play became more and more inappropriate. He lined up small toys, seemingly lost in intense attention to small details. He responded less and less to the presence of others in the room with him; people often seemed as objects to be used rather than beings with whom to relate. He didn't even revert to the early-toddler habit of pointing to something he wanted; which person was nearby—family member, friend, or acquaintance—was of little consequence.

Then near Christmas there came a moment of clarity. At the end of a long day of Christmas shopping we opted for fast food. We hurried the children from the car through the cold to face a restaurant full of exhausted families, long lines, and very few empty tables. We strategically positioned family members at the various stations: table, food line, utensils, etc. But when we prepared to sit down together for dinner, I saw Eric still standing near the counter, in the midst of the crowd but remarkably alone. I walked over to retrieve him and was struck not by what he said, but by what he could not say. Glancing up toward me but not making eye contact, and then pointing at a red glass ornament, he simply said, in a voice that had developed an inability to clearly enunciate its words, "Tree, ball." The extent of his language loss had become clear to me then: our son had only five words that he could use—none of them useful.

After the holidays, we ran Eric through what turned out to be an initial series of tests and then consultations. We ended up making, through the recommendation of our family doctor, an appointment with a hospital downtown that specialized in child-hood disorders. Chicago in late winter is not the most comfortable of places, especially for transplanted Californians, and on that morning of our appointment downtown, the air temperature was in the low forties, and a fine rain, threatening to turn into sleet, was being driven almost horizontally by the wind that blew off of Lake Michigan. We circled the hospital complex a couple of times, but the closest parking we could find was in a half-dirt alley partially covered by the track of the elevated train, in a space apparently abandoned by a morning commuter who had called it quits early that day. So we left with a walk of a couple of blocks, and, Eric, who had just turned three, was bundled up against the wind like a miniature of the Michelin Tire man in his oversized down jacket.

At the end of two days of testing, a young doctor called us in and asked if we had a sense of what was going on with our son. I said that a few nights ago we had seen a special on PBS depict-ing a little boy who seemed to dance in a world of his own—a lovely child who seemed unreachable behind an invisible wall. The program was on autism, and, after an awkward moment, the doctor confirmed that diagnosis and outlined the bleak prospects for Eric: little ability to develop emotional attachments, language limited by his condition, no chance for living an independent life. My wife had been considering a career in medicine; the doctor did not tell her just to put that idea on hold, but to abandon it. Eric, she said, would be Terry's job. The doctor spoke of a number of strategies for coping, but as she spoke, the room lost its focus. In that small consultation room, our world began to fall apart.

I remember one more scene. My dear wife was walking Eric around the house one night, pausing to point out object after object and patiently telling Eric the corresponding names, encouraging him to speak. Finally they paused at one of the living room windows. We were living on the second floor of a two-flat apartment that had originally been a single-family house, built in the early twentieth century by the landlord's father. The flat had handcrafted molding on the walls and ceilings and a bank of fine bay windows at the front. Outside it was a cloudy night, and the streetlight near our corner had gone out. We had read an account of an autistic boy who would point to any window, night or day, and say, "It's dark!"

A few days later we found Eric standing by the window on a beautiful sunny day, pointing at the glass and perhaps at the blue sky beyond. Terry and I walked over, and Eric did not acknowledge us. And our world had grown dark, indeed.

What do we do, particularly we professing Christians who claim to have been found by God and called to be lights in a dark world, when we come face to face with such deep darkness? What happens to our faith when our sense of God's plan or plot for our lives falls into what seems like senselessness? We live in a world with an increasingly postmodern mind-set that asks a more basic question: is the notion of plot in life a real possibility or something that we merely wish for?

A Boy with a Ruined Voice

Near my home in Chicago—"near" being defined as within five elevated train stops—was a particularly artist- and art-oriented area. There is a large music store/music school there of which I was quite fond; I love to play the guitar and have great respect for people who actually can play it well. This place was famous for bringing in more noncommercially-oriented acts into its small auditorium and for its countercultural, edgy clientele. I was browsing through the bookstore late one rainy afternoon, having completed my teaching for the day, when one of the store clerks (early twenties, a lot of piercings, tattoos) spied the book I had carried in from class. She then told me that the novel I held was her favorite book; it spoke to her and presented a plot that she could not read without being deeply moved. I have, in the years I have taught this novel, received similarly enthusiastic, glowing, unsolicited comments from people in all walks of life: I have never been the same, they all seem to say, since I read John Irving's *A Prayer for Owen Meany*.

Owen Meany is one of the strongest arguments I know of that this issue of whether life can have a plot is *not* neatly settled in our postmodern world. I have seen students, particularly, engaged with this book like few others. The novel begins,

> I am doomed to remember a boy with a wrecked voice—not because of his voice, or because he was the smallest person I ever knew, or because he was the instrument of my mother's death, but because he is the reason I believe in God; I am a Christian because of Owen Meany. (1)

What does this novel stir up in us? Just about all of us have lived through tragedies, and most of us who have realized that we are "wrecked" in some sense, that life and the world around us are not as they could be.

The very nature of John Irving's literary disposition places him in a fascinating position. Irving's major readership was launched by *The World According to Garp,* one of now five of his novels that have been turned into films. *Garp* is the story of a child's (and then a man's) constant struggle against the senselessness of life. And yet Irving cites, as the novel that caused him to want to be a writer, *Great Expectations* by Charles Dickens—a writer who never met a thoroughly intricate plot he didn't like. Irving has written the preface to an edition of the Dickens classic, mentions him in interviews as an important influence, and incorporates Dickens's *A Christmas Carol* into *A Prayer for Owen Meany.* But Owen Meany is a Christian literary character—in a world that has little patience for Christian terminology, plotted stories, stuffy morality, and claims to authority. The book possesses many traits that simply go against the cultural grain: ask any enthusiast of *Owen Meany,* who, unsuspecting, stumbled into a screening of *Simon Birch,* how the spiritual concerns of the novel fared in a film aimed at making a good return from a popular audience. The novel, however, doesn't flinch: it explores the tensions of voicing Christianity in a post-Christian age, not simply by introducing theological notions into an unwelcoming environment, but by embracing the struggle of Christian plot and human doubt as uncomfortable bedfellows.

The Tensions of Plot

The oddity of Owen Meany himself dominates the first third of the novel and its characters. And yet his strong presence and the connectedness of Irving's symbols seem to be at odds with another kind of character—the detached narrator, John—and the senselessness of the novel's initial events. So the novel sets up a classic battle between a character who knows that God has plotted his life and another person who is not so sure. That is, Owen and John themselves are at odds as representatives of the two ways of looking at life in our contemporary culture.

Owen Meany is a traditional protagonist—almost a nineteenth-century protagonist—who seems to awaken in a postmodern world. His otherworldliness reminds one of Dickens's sickly Oliver Twist, "an item of mortality" who needed to be encouraged "to take upon himself the office of respiration." Owen's otherworldliness, his ruined voice and abnormal smallness, evoke from the novel's other characters the shocked reaction of seeing something that is just not quite right—or not quite of this world. His diminutive self causes those around him to react as to a doll; they dress him up, they cannot help touching him, they play games in which Owen is hidden as a toy might be, and he even becomes the center of a game in Sunday school when he is passed around, "lifted up," held high overhead, his pockets emptied of baseball cards as he endures the game in silent fury.

But the whole package, in Owen's case, cannot be encountered as simply cute. When Owen introduces himself to John's wild cousins on the day after Thanksgiving, interrupting a typically chaotic scene in the attic by coming up unexpectedly through the trap door, the cousins react in ways that characters throughout the novel will react:

> . . . Owen Meany . . . stood with his hands clasped behind his back, the sun from the attic skylight shining through his protrusive ears, which were a glowing pink—the sunlight so bright that his tiny veins and blood vessels in his ears appeared to be illuminated from within. . . . [I]n that blaze of sunlight he looked

like a gnome plucked fresh from a fire, with his ears still aflame.
I drew in my breath, and Hester—with her raging mouth full of
purple thread—looked up at that instant and saw Owen, too.
She screamed. (69)

Owen always draws a reaction, whether his appearance is inter-
preted as Christ figure, fiery god, evil spirit, or something akin
to a living lawn gnome. As John's grandmother states, when
describing mice whose necks have been broken in their house's
mousetraps, "that boy's voice could bring those mice back to
life" (17). So one might say that Owen Meany represents the
many contradictory images of a contemporary Christian: cute
and abnormal, sacred and frightening, laughable and effective—a
boy who, rather than calling forth Lazarus, nowadays could only
call forth mice from their little tombs. And so, through these images, Irving presents an essential tension: Owen Meany is to be
taken either as a "little Christ" or as the representative of a faith
reduced by the contemporary world to something that seems a
caricature of its former self.

Set beside Owen for comparison is a picture of ambiguity, anxiety, and disorientation: John Wheelwright, the novel's
protagonist. He is the book's nonperson, displaced and disabled, who stands apart from the action to be the observer
of senseless violence, and who stands at the center of plots
that never quite pan out. He stands as a mute witness to his
mother's untimely and unnatural death. He is disabled both in
his reading abilities and his sexuality—he is once described by
a friend's husband as a "non-practicing homosexual," meaning that John doesn't "know what he is." He lives out his life
as an expatriate in Toronto, teaching English in an all-girl's
Anglican prep school. He can never be accepted as really Canadian, because he cannot let go of his anger about American

foreign policy and the Vietnam War. He is absent even when he is with his own family: his mother seems to pay more attention to Owen than to him, the identity of his father remains a mystery for the greater portion of the novel, and even his own grandmother, in her senility, cannot remember who he is—but remembers Owen Meany. John is best positioned as Owen's sidekick—someone who keeps Owen company, someone whose significant actions are always directed by Owen (be it Owen's creation of a window by which John overcomes his dyslexia and reads Hardy, or Owen's decision to cut off a portion of John's finger in order to keep John from being drafted into the army). John Wheelwright as a young boy is cast in the nativity play as Joseph, and indeed is cast in this role for life: he is the bystander in the divine story, the one who so quickly drops out of the picture that the Gospel writers do not bother to record the time or circumstances of his death, the one who, both in the Gospels and in *A Prayer for Owen Meany*, often shows his faith by not taking action.

But the juxtaposition of John and Owen leads the reader not to question John, but to question Owen. Although Owen is acknowledged by almost all as bright and gifted, the tensions surrounding the cast of characters' assessment of him center on his religious life and his sense of calling—of plot. John's cousin Hester—Owen's live-in partner during college—becomes so enraged that she pins him to the floor in his apartment and beats his face until she draws blood, because of his insistence that his life has been plotted by God. Both John's stepfather and his real father express two doubting critiques of Owen's sense of plot. The first credits Owen's sense of plot to the latter's keen intellect; that is, a bright person can make plot and connections where none really exist. The second's objections are based more on the promotion of doubt as a sort of faith, reflective perhaps of the sort of faith espoused by Irving's mentor, Frederick Buechner, quoted in the novel before its title page:

> Not the least of my problems is that I can hardly even imagine what kind of an experience a genuine, self-authenticating religious experience would be. Without somehow destroying me in the process, how could God reveal himself in a way that would leave no room for doubt? If there were no room for doubt, there would be no room for me.

The most violent and lasting of the reactions to Owen, however, is that of Hester, who builds a songwriting career based on her anger at Owen Meany's commitment to plot. Hester rails at Owen (and still rails at him even in his absence), because of her dismissal of the idea that he is "plotted" to sacrifice himself for others. For Hester, no God, no "Author" is present to give the basis or to define the cause for such a sacrifice. A sampling of her song titles says as much: "No Church, No Country, No More," "Just Another Dead Hero," "I Don't Believe in No Soul." And after the incident in which Hester pounds Owen because of his fidelity to God's plot, John's narration and Owen's statement outline the problem:

> . . . his nose had stopped bleeding, but his lip was split quite deeply—it continued to bleed—and there was a sizable swelling above one of his eyebrows. He had two black eyes, one very much blacker than the other and so puffy that the eye was closed to a slit.
> "YOU THINK VIETNAM IS DANGEROUS," he said. "YOU OUGHT TO TRY LIVING WITH *HESTER!*"
> But he was so exasperating! How could *anyone* live with Owen Meany and, knowing what he thought he knew, *not* be moved to beat the s— out of him? (422)

And so the battle lines of the novel are often drawn: is life real plot or only wishful contrivance? By the end of the book's first three chapters, the reader is offered this vision: Owen Meany is a little director of lives, and as such is either one who is attempting to be true to an invisible God, or one who is grasping for control. The novel can be read in either of these two ways; maybe the ambiguity is what appeals to the contemporary reader who both longs for and is wary of: the idea that life can have a plot.

Owen Meany as a Proponent of Plot

For a moment, let us say that *A Prayer for Owen Meany* is a conventional novel—a lost Dickens idea that emerges and develops in the late twentieth century. We would recognize such a book, even though we might be surprised to find one written during this period, by its use of symbols, the authoritative voice of its lead character, and ultimately a story that comes to closure. And so for a long moment we will excuse John and Hester and the complications they bring to our efforts and concentrate on Owen Meany himself as the novel's reliable hero.

First, every good Dickens novel, and every life seen as having a plot, needs its symbol. One finds it introduced early, innocently enough, but as the novel continues and the plot thickens, one trips over the symbol like one of those tree roots that keep emerging in the backyard, the sort that first buckles the walkway and eventually wreaks havoc on the garage's cement foundation. The symbol can be thought of as an iceberg, and the reader as the *Titanic*. What seemed like a minor cause for detour ends up as the end of the story itself.

The dominant symbol of Owen Meany is introduced, innocently enough, during an offhand description of the local history of Gravesend, New Hampshire, barely into the first chapter.

> The local sagamore's [chief's] name was Watahantowet; instead of his signature, he made his mark upon the deed in the form of his totem—an armless man. Later, there was some dispute—not very interesting—regarding the Indian deed, and more interesting speculation regarding *why* Watahantowet's totem was an armless man. Some said it was how it made the sagamore feel to give up all that land—to have his arms cut off—and others pointed out that . . . the figure, although armless, held a feather in his mouth; this was said to indicate the sagamore's frustration at being unable to write. But in several other versions of the totem ascribed to Watahantowet, the figure has a tomahawk in its mouth and looks completely crazy—or else, he is making a gesture toward peace: no arms, tomahawk in mouth; together, perhaps, they are meant to signify that Watahantowet does not fight. As for the settlement of the disputed deed, you can be sure the Indians were *not* the beneficiaries of the resolution to that difference of opinion. (19)

Watahantowet's totem emerges in various forms in the novel. Armlessness or dismemberment is a theme (as it is in *Garp*) and is played out in Owen's gift of a disfigured, petrified armadillo as an act of apology and explanation to John over the death of his mother; in the armless dressmaker's dummy that becomes Owen's substitute for Tabby Wheelwright; in the disassembling of the "holy goalie" (the statue of Mary Magdalene that Owen displaces from the gate of the Catholic school and then places, dismembered, on the stage of the assembly hall in protest of his expulsion from Gravesend Academy).

But, of course, the symbol becomes the event that forces one to reinterpret the novel—the death that Owen Meany is plotted to die at the end of the story. A psychopath tosses a grenade into a restroom that holds seven small Vietnamese children, John Wheelwright, and Owen Meany, and in Owen's act of heroism, in saving the children, Owen Meany, grabbing the grenade and, being lifted up by John, using his own arms as a shelter against the blast, becomes armless.

> "NOW I KNOW WHY YOU HAD TO BE HERE," Owen said to me. "DO YOU SEE WHY?" he asked me.
> "Yes," I said.
> "REMEMBER ALL OUR PRACTICING?" he asked me.
> "I remember," I said.
> Owen tried to raise his hands; he tried to reach out to me with his arms—I think he wanted to touch me. That was when he realized that his arms were gone. He didn't seem surprised by the discovery.
> "REMEMBER WATAHANTOWET?" he asked me.
> "I remember," I said.
> Then he smiled at the [nun] who was trying to make him comfortable in her lap; her wimple was covered with his blood, and she had wrapped as much of her habit around him as she could manage—because he was shivering.
> " '. . . WHOSOEVER LIVETH AND BELIEVETH IN ME SHALL NEVER DIE,' " Owen said to her. The nun nodded in agreement; she made the sign of the cross over him. (615)

At this point, everything in the novel has become meaningful. Suddenly, Owen Meany fulfills the symbol that Watahantowet is introduced to be. Owen is armless, and chooses not to fight the plot in which he finds himself. His armlessness is a sign of peace, saving the children who are victims of their country's war and, John would add, America's military craziness. Like Watahantowet, Owen is perceived (by Hester and his family) as completely crazy, but the end of the novel proves them wrong. One then remembers all the times of Owen's armlessness as foreshadowing events: his arms folded tightly as he is lifted up in Sunday school, or when he is hidden by Hester in their games as children, or when Hester beats him by sitting on his chest and pinning his arms to the floor with her knees. Owen's previously inexplicable fear of nuns becomes clear in their association with the scene of his death; the necessity of his damaged voice and his diminutive size is evident in the need for the Vietnamese children to listen to him and not fear him; the purpose of the years of practicing the basketball shot with John in which John lifts Owen up to dunk the ball is made clear in the ultimate act. One is reminded of all the lifting up that takes place in the novel, and of Christ's statement, equally inexplicable when spoken in John's Gospel, but understood in light of the crucifixion and ascension, "When I am lifted up, I will draw the whole world to me."

Owen Meany as a believer in plot often speaks with a prophetic voice—the voice that speaks truth to both power and self-deception. He speaks to just about anyone in a position of authority in the novel. Notably, Owen speaks through the school's newspaper to Randy White, the business-minded dean of Gravesend Academy, who secularizes the chapel and whose aim is to secure his own power above the interest of those he "serves." Owen speaks to the Reverend Merrill on issues of faith and the reverend's lack thereof, the results of which are heard through Merrill's eulogy at Owen Meany's funeral. But perhaps Owen's most authoritative moment is when he usurps the annual nativity play and places himself in the cradle as the Christ child.

Such plays are safe events—cuteness and light embodied in the voices of seven-year-olds dressed as shepherds, angels, and wise men. The scenes are played out before parents with video cameras, before relatives who during the year may never set foot in the church. These plays have taken on a story of their own, embellishing the actually austere biblical accounts of the nativity. Owen Meany, who wrestles direction of the play from the Episcopalian rector's wife and parish power monger, Barb Wiggin, sets out to change all that. Owen intends to make the audience understand the need of the angel's original admonition, "Be not afraid."

After "correcting" several of the staging errors, and choosing his Mary and his Joseph—John Wheelwright, of course—Owen Meany casts himself as the baby Jesus. He is, after all, someone small enough to fit in a cradle, and someone who won't engage in that disorderly crying during what should be a serious play. In the interest of time, Reverend Wiggin omits the fourth verse of "We Three Kings," effectively ending the nativity hymn with "Sorrowing, sighing, bleeding, dying, sealed in a stone-cold tomb." In the play that Owen "directs," the crèche of hay is completed upon the conclusion of this verse, upon which the baby Jesus, wrapped in swaddling clothes, is placed in the center of the spotlighted scene:

> Why we didn't just wrap him in a blanket, I don't know. The "swaddling clothes" resembled nothing so much as layers upon layers of gauze bandages, so that Owen resembled some terrifying burn victim who'd been shriveled to abnormal size in a fire that had left only his face and arms uncharred—and the "pillar of light," and the worshipful postures of all of us, surrounding him, made it appear that Owen was about to undergo some ritual unwrapping in an operating room. . . . (157)

What Owen looks like, as the fourth line of the hymn points out, is Christ laid in the tomb, not the baby Jesus in the manger. During the production, which now can only be described as a nativity play for adults, or an Advent event that anticipates

Jesus's sacrifice in the crucifixion, Owen Meany directs the other actors by "whispering" forgotten lines—something impossible to do quietly given his injured voice—so that the baby Jesus develops a speaking part. The play goes awry, and Owen, who has become something like "a commanding officer surveying his troops," surveys the congregation and discovers two unwanted guests: his father and mother. What follows must be read to be appreciated.

> Owen sat up so suddenly on the mountain of hay that several front-pew members of the congregation were startled into gasps and cries of alarm. He bent stiffly at the waist, like a tightly wound spring, and he pointed with ferocity at his mother and father; to many members of the congregation, he could have been pointing to anyone—or to them all.
>
> "WHAT DO YOU THINK *YOU'RE* DOING HERE?" the angry Lord Jesus screamed.
>
> Many members of the congregation thought he meant *them*; I could tell what a shock the question was for Mr. Fish [who was not a churchgoer], but I knew whom Owen was speaking to. I saw Mr. and Mrs. Meany cringe; they slipped off the pew to the kneeling pad, and Mrs. Meany covered her face with both hands.
>
> "YOU SHOULDN'T BE HERE!" Owen shouted at them; but Mr. Fish, and surely half the congregation, felt that *they* stood accused. I saw the faces of the Rev. Lewis Merrill and his California wife; it was apparent that they also thought Owen Meany meant *them*.
>
> "IT IS A *SACRILEGE* FOR YOU TO BE HERE!" Owen hollered. At least a dozen members of the congregation guiltily got up from the pews at the rear of the church—to leave. (200)

After recounting the incident, John states,

How can you like Christmas after that? Before I became a believer,
I could at least enjoy the fantasy. (206)

But Owen, despite the dark comedy of the action, reinvests the
cute nativity play with meaning, through the authority of his
voice. Flannery O'Connor once stated that the goal of the Christian writer was to return her audience to reality at all costs, to
not allow an audience the protection of a self-constructed facade
that would let the gospel be civilized into something comfortable
and thus inapplicable to one's own sins.

But it is interesting to note the unintended consequences of
Owen's direction as well, as he means to speak to his parents but
additionally convicts those others in the audience who perhaps
have forgotten that they have wandered not into an assembly, into
a nice Christmas tradition, but into a *church*. These unintentional
results throughout the novel, when Plot, if you will, overrides
Owen's plot, are Owen Meany's most effective moments. It is
this Plot, and not Owen's (who consistently attempts, and fails,
to direct his own destiny) that gives the novel such a sense of
finality and closure in Owen's sacrificial death.

The Other Side: *A Prayer for Owen Meany* as a Novel of Doubt

But, for a moment, let us say that *A Prayer for Owen Meany*
is a novel of doubt, a book that argues against life having a plot.
We would recognize such a book by its use of symbols that ultimately go nowhere (or to many different places), by the tentative
voice of its lead character, and by a story that resists a neat, clean
ending. And so for another long moment we will excuse Owen
Meany—something that certainly no character in the novel did
very successfully—in order to concentrate on John and Hester.

Let's first return to the initial description of Watahantowet:

The local sagamore's name was Watahantowet; instead of his signature, he made his mark upon the deed in the form of his totem—an armless man. Later, there was some dispute—not very interesting—regarding the Indian deed, and more interesting speculation regarding *why* Watahantowet's totem was an armless man. Some said it was how it made the sagamore feel to give up all that land—to have his arms cut off—and others pointed out that . . . the figure, although armless, held a feather in his mouth; this was said to indicate the sagamore's frustration at being unable to write. But in several other versions of the totem ascribed to Watahantowet, the figure has a tomahawk in its mouth and looks completely crazy—or else, he is making a gesture toward peace: no arms, tomahawk in mouth; together, perhaps, they are meant to signify that Watahantowet does not fight. (19)

A set of readers might see Watahantowet as John: he gives up his land and moves to Canada (and one should remember that he does not have to—Owen's surgery takes care of his draft exemption), but he cannot give up his anger over his country of origin; his dyslexia leaves him frustrated in the acts of reading and writing, even though he will become an English instructor; his gesture toward peace is "the tomahawk in his mouth"—that is, John's words in the Canada sections of the novel violently rail against the foreign policy of Ronald Reagan; and, John does not fight. Indeed, John's life is characterized by a passive acceptance of his "Joseph-ness." He does not fight Owen Meany's sense of destiny; he does not fight for much of anything for himself.

Or Watahantowet could be Hester. She is constantly on the "Indian" end of any deal the novel gives her: her brothers are given opportunities, while Hester has to settle; the one love of her life is taken away from her in an agreement (between God and Owen) that she cannot comprehend; when the cousins play chasing games as children, the *loser* has to kiss Hester. The tomahawk in her mouth is reminiscent of the wild action of her mouth on the thread as Owen first bursts into the attic before Thanksgiving. And the violence of her mouth is her songs; wailing, angry *peace* songs. Hester will not fight.

And the symbol can become more confused. A sagamore in the novel is not just the name of Watahantowet, the chief of a once-local tribe, it is also the proper name given by Mr. Fish (without any clear sense of its origins and meaning) to his dog—a dog who, in pursuit of a football that Owen Meany accidentally kicks well, is killed by a diaper truck. What could be more senseless?

Irving writes, as if to challenge his own symbol,

> As always, with Owen Meany, there was the necessary consideration of the *symbols* involved. He had removed Mary Magdalene's arms, above the elbows, so that her gesture of beseeching the assembled audience would seem all the more an act of supplication—and all the more helpless. Dan and I both knew that Owen suffered from an obsession with armlessness—this was Watahantowet's familiar totem, this was what Owen had done to my armadillo. My mother's dressmaker's dummy was armless, too.
>
> But neither Dan nor I was prepared for Mary Magdalene being *headless*—for her head was cleanly sawed or chiseled or blasted off. Because my mother's dummy was also headless, I thought that Mary Magdalene bore her a stony three- or four-hundred-pound resemblance. (357)

Why does Owen Meany, careful crafter of symbols, make Mary Magdalene headless? Is it to relate her, for some reason, to Tabby Wheelwright? But why put Tabby on stage next to Randy White? Is the headlessness a cruel joke on the school lacking a real headmaster, or a prophecy of White's firing? Is there a plot, or just random chance?

In a way of asking this question, the novel's back-to-back pageants, the nativity play and a local production of Dickens's *Christmas Carol,* seem to juxtapose the authoritative voice of Owen Meany, the Christ child, with the voiceless Owen Meany, the finger-pointing ghost of Christmas future. The contrast is striking. Owen is still remarkably effective in a role that (thank goodness) remains a nonspeaking part, but the contrast of the Ghost of Christmas Yet to Come—a ghost that can offer Ebenezer Scrooge no assurance of a future plot line but only choices—to the authoritative Christ child, whose life is ultimately plotted, cannot be clearer. Irving writes of the performance:

> I did not need to see him to know he was there. A hush fell over the audience. The faces of my fellow townspeople—so amused, so curious, so various—were rendered shockingly similar . . . the identity of Owen Meany was [not] clear; what was clear was that he *was* a ghost. . . .
>
> Owen coughed. It was not, as Dan Needham had hoped, a "humanizing" sound; it was a rattle so deep, and so deeply associated with death, that the audience was startled—people twitched in their seats. . . . That was when I turned to look at him—at the instant his baby-powdered hand shot out of the black folds of his cowl, and he pointed. A fever chill sent a spasm down his trembling arm, and his hand responded to the jolt as to electricity. Mr. Fish flinched. (219–20)

Finally, *Owen Meany,* if viewed as a novel that sees the world as ultimately plotless, leaves us only with Owen's death and absence. John and Hester are deeply affected by the lingering sense of Owen's absence and live strikingly parallel existences in his absence. They both live lives of sexual loneliness, Hester through her conquest of a plethora of underaged lovers but no partner to replace Owen, and John the eunuch with a plethora of underaged students who are "completely safe in his presence." Both verbally rail at Owen's absence: Hester through her Owen-haunted songs, John through his diatribes against America that make him "too angry to be accepted as a Canadian"—he is haunted by America. Both are damaged goods, without hope of regaining what they now lack: Owen, and a sense that their lives have meaning. They are spiritual amputees.

A Resolution: John's Testimony

At the end of the novel, John Wheelwright seems to be wrong about the role cast for him by Owen Meany. He is not merely a Joseph, he is also John: the disciple Christ loved, the one left in exile on Patmos and in old age to bear witness to Christ who is risen but who now is physically absent. What results from John's testimony of his life during and after the intrusion into it by Owen, the "little Christ," is at times very unsatisfying, but is a faith nonetheless.

The action that leads to John's personal resolution is one of the last acts of direction by Owen Meany. Whereas Owen is a little Christ, perhaps a model on his best days of a valid Christian acting out of faith in a world that is wary of Christianity, John can only be a little Owen. Owen claims that God has taken away his hands; John can only claim that Owen has taken away his finger. Owen removes the trigger finger above the first knuckle, thus not only dismissing John from military duty but leaving him with a visible reminder of his relationship to Owen Meany. And slowly, John, in writing his testimony, becomes a sort of Owen; his Canadian voice and the missives he writes on American foreign policy from his exile are reminiscent of Owen's prophetic work as The Voice in the Gravesend Academy newspaper—he even begins to sound like Owen at times.

The faith that John finds is best described in one of the last of Owen's lessons for John on how faith works.

> When it was so dark at St. Michael's playground that we couldn't see the basket, we couldn't see Mary Magdalene, either. What Owen liked best was to practice the shot until we lost Mary Magdalene in the darkness. Then he would stand under the basket with me and say, "CAN YOU SEE HER?"
>
> "Not anymore," I'd say.
>
> "YOU CAN'T SEE HER, BUT YOU KNOW SHE'S STILL THERE—RIGHT?" he would say.
>
> "Of course she's still there!" I'd say . . . .
>
> "BUT YOU CAN'T *SEE* HER," he'd say—very teasingly. "HOW DO YOU KNOW SHE'S STILL THERE IF YOU CAN'T ACTUALLY SEE HER?"
>
> "Because I *know* she's still there—because I know she couldn't have gone anywhere . . ."
>
> "WELL, NOW YOU KNOW HOW I FEEL ABOUT GOD," said Owen Meany. (399–400)

In our darkest times—in my *darkest* times—it seems appropriate to describe faith as practicing the shot in the dark, acting out faith in an atmosphere that seems to be full of doubt and plotlessness, but knowing that God and his plot for our lives are still very much there.

I think we are mistaken, however, if we consider the problem of whether life has a plot, so poignantly described in *A Prayer for Owen Meany,* as a "new" problem—something unique to our age. In fact, distrusting claims that something is new is a healthy response. The Gospels, written now close to 2,000 years ago in a culture so different from our own, seem very familiar with our "contemporary" problems.

> In our darkest times—in my *darkest* times—it seems appropriate to describe faith as practicing the shot in the dark, acting out faith in an atmosphere that seems to be full of doubt and plotlessness, but knowing that God and his plot for our lives are still very much there.

The twelfth chapter of John's Gospel is full of questions about truth and plot. According to the account, Jesus is dining with some friends, one of whom, it just so happens, is reported to have been raised from the dead. Now, that's an unexpected plot twist! The friend, Lazarus, has become an attraction. A crowd has arrived: some have come to see Lazarus (who wouldn't?); some religious leaders of the day are so upset about the effect this story has had on the people that they plan to kill both Jesus and Lazarus; others are in denial—with the recently dead man at the table, one disciple is arguing about the cost of a "wasted" bottle of expensive perfume. Perhaps a few believe; in any case, it's all rather unsettling.

Jesus then ups the stakes by riding into Jerusalem on a young colt at the beginning of a public holiday—in doing so he is fulfilling a prophecy about how the Messiah will arrive in Jerusalem, and this is not lost on the crowd who sees him. They yell, "Blessed is the King of Israel!" (John 12:13). Then, as Jesus prays publicly in the middle of the feast, John writes that a voice answers him from the heavens. The response? "The crowd that was there and heard it said it had thundered; others say an angel had spoken to him" (John 12:29). In other words, some responded by saying, "I know what you think you heard, but your truth is not necessarily my truth."

This is not an isolated incident—such actions and claims and reactions run through the Bible's four Gospel accounts. Near the beginning of the book of Mark, in its third chapter, Jesus is in a local place of worship when he completely restores the shriveled hand of a man in the congregation. The religious leaders are upset enough with his apparent lack of respect for the law and his implied claim about who he is to plot his death. They shortly take another strategy and accuse Jesus not of being God, but of being the devil. But the crowds that gather become so large that many people, including Jesus's own family, become frightened. They reason together that he must be out of his mind and come to take him home to a normal, quiet life where deformed people are not made whole again and crowds don't call an ordinary person "king" and religious leaders don't try to kill off the opposition. This, I think, must have been one of the most difficult moments Jesus went through, when his own family allowed their fear to stifle their faith in him. But Jesus is convinced of the plot that God his Father has given him. He chooses to follow his confidence in being the Messiah who will live and reign forever, to believe the plot even when his friends and family turn away, when the curious are curious no longer, when those who want to remove the threat he represents seem to get their way.

To believe in this kind of plot means believing that God does intervene in lives and history, especially in the particular case of Jesus of Nazareth. And those of us who believe, who call ourselves Christians (literally, "little Christs"), expect God to intervene in our lives, in the lives of those around us, and in history. This is not a postmodern view, because thinking of plot in this way, and thinking that such plots affect others and not only ourselves, moves us out of the realm of contextual truth (it's truth for you in your world, but not for me in my world) into absolute truth. To think of oneself as a "little Christ" may tempt one's family and friends to come around and try to take one back to a normal life, where we don't bother one another with intrusive claims of truth and God's plots for our lives. The decision to be made today, in this "postmodern" world, seems very similar to the decisions that had to be made in the "ancient" world. Is plot, in this seemingly plotless world, real or invented? Does God intervene in the natural world? Are the claims that Jesus made legitimated by a voice from heaven, or are they just empty thunder?

I can report to you my own witness, like John Wheelwright's witness to Owen Meany, about plot.

About a year before we received my son's diagnosis, I experienced one of three moments in my life when I had an evident, doubtless sense of God's direction. My wife and I were both living in exhaustion: we were both in graduate school and raising two children with few resources; we wanted to have a third child but were not sure if we could raise another child and care for Eric. So we agreed to pray about the situation. The answer I received in prayer from God was an almost audible yes, jarring in its strength and clarity. I wondered about the timing.

The third son born to us has been instrumental in my second son's healing. My wife and I saw that, time and time again in Eric's critical early years just after the diagnosis, his little brother walked him through the missed developmental steps in a way that no one else could.

Not everyone agrees with this view, by the way. When Eric began to get better—to improve beyond all reason (he is social, loving, caring, mature, other-centered)—some of those close to us suggested that the initial diagnosis must have been wrong, or that we are just particularly good parents. Well, there are many good parents who don't see tragedies turn around, and at the time of his diagnosis, Eric satisfied ten of the twelve markers for autism, well above the "required" number. My experience tells me that God is still there, even in the darkness of life when

I can no longer sense his presence. And I know that such faith in him and his plot for me will be repeatedly tested, and I don't know what stage of the journey I will be in at any given time. But I know that there is plot in this plotless world, and that after night, there is joy in the morning.

{ 4 }

Connecting with Christ's Vision—Finding Real Plot in the Age of Me

What are the expectations for living a Christian life? Shortly after I became a Christian, I made God and myself a promise: I would read at least one chapter of the Bible a day for a year. Sometimes I did more, reading from both the Old and New Testaments, but this was my baseline. I don't think it was based in legalism: instead, I had experienced the Bible as an "interactive text"—a way of hearing from God and then responding to him in prayer, a conversation of sorts. The words I would receive from that book had more of an effect on me than just "conversation"—I did draw from them a sense of being with God, but also a sense of an ability to change. And I knew that quite a lot about my life, and about who I was on the inside, needed changing.

I think it was about six months into this process that I began to have questions about plot—about what God wanted for my life, and about how I knew I was on the right track. The lives I encountered in the Bible were full of meaning. Sometimes the events I encountered were great moments in a life and sometimes painful ones, but what I encountered were lives charged with plot: David, Jacob, Esther, Ruth, Solomon, Paul, Jesus himself. The notion of having a meaningful life, and the expectation that real Christians by their nature should be experiencing such lives, was reinforced each Sunday from the pulpit, and by writers I encountered who had written on the Christian life, and by other speakers I heard on the radio. But my life seemed to be different from what I heard and read, and I suspected something was wrong.

I regularly experienced the high points of the Christian life: insight, change, a sense of God's presence and spirit, the delights of worship and of being with other believers. But although I did not experience many "lows" of a Christian life, I often seemed to experience "lacks." That is, most of the events of my days and my weeks had little to do with Christian highs and lows. My work was just work, I experienced the same annoyances of day-to-day life as everyone else—bills, car repairs, the joys of sitting on the freeway during the morning commute with thousands of strangers.

But there were other aspects of my life that were more troubling for someone expecting a life of meaning. There were hours in my life that simply needed filling in, and I wasn't exactly sure what the proper "Christian" ways of doing that were. This may sound strange to the more well-adjusted folks among my readers, but this was an issue for me. When I became a Christian, my life underwent a profound change—my world turned upside down—and I did not know what items from my old life were proper to carry into my new life.

Moreover, as a writer—for someone interested in literature, art, and music generally—there were not many models or even sympathetic sets of directions in the evangelical world. A carpenter's work or hobbies would not be under question, but a Christian who is a writer or an artist seems to many other Christians as someone who produces things of either questionable value or potentially dangerous effect. Moreover, my life still had holes. There were times when I was lonely, when Christian fellowship ran into the same limitations of any friendship or relationship in a busy world where human interaction is often shortchanged in favor of a "things-to-accomplish" list. At my conversion my life had gained great meaning—I had a sense of God's plot, of the big issues, of why we lived and for whom we lived and of being transformed by Christ on the inside. I was just having trouble with life's details.

As I continued to read the Bible, I came to a conclusion about the "lack" I was feeling in my day-to-day life. I realized that I had placed myself into a game of unfair comparisons in which I could never really compete. True, I was reading about wonderful lives in the Bible, lives that taught me lessons and gave me models for thinking and living. But I was reading compressed accounts of lives—the greatest hits, if you will. The Acts of the Apostles condenses years of missionary journeys, drawing out from the stories those events important to the history of the church or its doctrine. Even the very human accounts of the lives of Jacob and Joseph, which certainly cover the highs and lows of their lives, still tell only the major events. As I thought about my Christian life, I became more puzzled with that part of life that makes up the majority of our time on earth: the day-to-day. What should this time be like for me? Should the details be filled with meaning?

> People seem to be driven to move from house to house, or job to job, in search of measurable success. What happens in between those successes?

As I continued to read the Old and New Testaments, I realized that there were other voices in God's records that seemed to ask the same questions: Ecclesiastes, Proverbs, and the Psalms addressed these issues. And the apostle Paul was keenly aware of them, advising those in the early church of the value of working with one's hands, and the necessity of occupying until the Lord returned. The stakes in these matters became high ones for me. I saw a portion of the Christian community that spent a surprising amount of time hanging around church: they were there during the weekends and during the week for Bible studies and prayer meetings. But between this schedule and the demands of their jobs, what time was left for other responsibilities such as family and friendships? What time was left for other things in life that brought them joy? I wondered: were my fellow Christians swept up in the "greatest hits" expectations for life that I had found, and were they trying to somehow live out events like those on a daily basis? If that was the model of the Christian life, what did that mean about the rest of living in this world? Did it mean that God valued only the great moments and had little to say to us about all he had put on earth for our care and enjoyment?

I would like to suggest that this is not just a problem for Christians. Our culture seems focused on the issues of "the greatest hits" as well. People seem to be driven to move from house to house, or job to job, in search of measurable success. What happens in between those successes? Is day-to-day life just a means for getting us to the "highs" and for avoiding the "lows," or is there value and substance in the day-to-day itself?

Solomon's Struggle with the Daily Grind

Every family has a member that needs some explanation. Some have two or three. That is, if you plan to host a get-together in which people outside of the family are there, then someone is usually in charge of giving an explanation about an eccentric brother, or an aunt who just seems a little outside the mold. We are fairly certain that this family member will, if no explanation is offered, make the newcomer uncomfortable. We are without a doubt that this is the effect on us.

Solomon, king of Israel, represents the kingdom and the kingship at its brief zenith. The record reports that he built the temple, collected about twenty-five *tons* per year of gold in tribute, decorated his palaces with gold and ivory, had a fleet of trading ships, expanded Israel's territory, and greatly increased its respect among its neighbors. His wisdom, not just his wealth, was a wonder of the world. When God tells Solomon that he will give him whatever he would like, Solomon replies, "Give me wisdom and knowledge, that I may lead this people . . ." (2 Chron. 1:10). God replies that because Solomon did not ask for the things kings might ask for—wealth, honor, the deaths of his enemies, or even for a long life—God will give him not only wisdom and knowledge, but wealth and honor such as no king has ever received. And so, by the end of his life, Solomon "made silver as common in Jerusalem as stones" (1 Kings 10:27).

As his successes accumulate, however, Solomon's pride grows. He builds places of worship to other gods, adversaries arise, infighting erupts, and the kingdom begins its long fall from zenith to nadir.

We suspect that the Old Testament book of Ecclesiastes, attributed to Solomon, is written after the decline begins. It seems to be the most pessimistic book of the Bible, as its sayings are

> Life is full of randomness—the good suffer, the evil prosper, and those who work hard may in the end lose it all.

delivered from someone for whom God's wisdom, in a sense, has become a curse: he is the wisest man in the world and therefore can see the enormity of his mistakes. And so this book becomes our own "eccentric uncle," the book that doesn't seem to fit in with the rest, the book about which we desire to make excuses and explanations before people who are new to the Bible read it and get "the wrong idea."

The first two chapters of the book are devastating. In them, the following human activities and values ultimately bring pain: beauty, because it becomes tiresome; wisdom, because when human behavior is understood, it brings one grief; seeking pleasure through undertaking projects, acquisition, and by simply experiencing as much as one can, because it all proves to be meaningless; differentiating between wise and mad living, because they both end in death. The book goes on to decry advancement without wisdom, envy, work and wealth without fellowship, riches, and children—all of which by themselves offer no assurance of happiness. Ecclesiastes proclaims that oppression is the way of the world, and one should be not at all surprised when he or she observes the oppression of the weak or the absence of justice from the poor, because ultimately kings rule for themselves. Life is full of randomness—the good suffer, the evil prosper, and those who work hard may in the end lose it all. Then Solomon, the family's downbeat uncle who at this point in his life was probably not invited to family celebrations, comes to a conclusion: Have enough wisdom to not get carried away with life and instead remember God, because ultimately you will arrive before him to have your life judged; and, he proclaims, "it is good and proper for a man to eat and drink, and to find satisfaction in his toilsome labor under the sun during the few days of life God has given him—for this is his lot. Moreover, when God gives any man wealth and possessions, and enables him to enjoy them, to accept his lot and be happy in his work—this is a gift of God" (Eccles. 5:18–19).

What is Solomon saying? That life is pointless? That the universe is cold and cruel and random? That one ought to enjoy pleasures when one can? That it's best not to look too deeply into things lest one become despondent? I'll be quite blunt: during Sunday morning services, the scripture for the day is not often taken from these portions of Ecclesiastes. Solomon is a bit like the person who stands up in the midst of the pep rally and reminds us that our players aren't really all that good. He comes to the party to celebrate the purchase of the new home and points out the dark mold on the outside wall near the back door. He's the person who comes to the Sunday morning service and reminds those who go forward that this isn't going to solve all their problems. This may all be true, we think, but do we have to talk about it *now*?

Ecclesiastes invites us to enter into a conversation with God and one another, and it is exactly the conversation that I wanted to have, before I became a Christian, with believers. Sometimes I go through seasons in my life when I still want to have it. Is there such a thing as a meaningful life? If God exists, then why do I see such misery and randomness in the world? Is there anything I can do to make my life complete and whole? The literature of our day proves that this conversation still cries out to be engaged in our culture, and I think in our churches as well. As I stated, as a new convert I asked, "God, I understand the big plan, but what of the details of my life? Does a plot extend there as well?" Solomon's answer to this is an eye-opener. As we have seen, Solomon endorses enjoying what one has been given in the fellowship of one's friends. He advises to not be hasty with words and judgments, because "God is in heaven and you are on earth"—in other words, our perspective is limited and God's is not. And at the end of chapter 7 of Ecclesiastes, Solomon states:

> This only have I found: God made mankind upright, but men have gone in search of many schemes. (Eccles. 7:29)

I believe that what Solomon concludes is so central to our own problems that it is worth immediate pause, study, and conversation. But in order to better see its relevance in today's world, and to understand that the church is not the only party asking these questions, I want us to enter into a conversation with a popular film that might first seem an unlikely participant: *Groundhog Day*.

In Search of Many Schemes

At the height of his popularity, Bill Murray starred in *Groundhog Day*, a film which in its first twenty minutes has all the marks of a typical Murray protagonist: arrogance, sarcasm, and a tendency to be funny in spite of himself. Murray as Phil is a second-market television weatherman who believes he has never been properly appreciated and thus has been passed over for promotion into the first tier; therefore, as he continues his work in Pittsburgh, he becomes less secure about his own future and a bit more trouble to work with—a "prima donna" as his cameraman puts it. To rub salt into the wounds, he is forced to work for an idealistic, younger, female producer, whose optimism and cheerfulness he has little patience for. Phil, Rita (the producer), and the cameraman travel to Punxsutawney, Pennsylvania, for their annual spot on Groundhog Day, in which Phil must report on the findings of his counterpart, groundhog Punxsutawney Phil, and the latter's prognosis for the continuing winter. Phil the weatherman, who spends the night before in an upscale bed-and-breakfast, leaving his companions to a local chain hotel, goes through the motions with considerable sharpness. The three leave town not the best of friends, but are stopped by a snowstorm (which Phil had confidently predicted would miss them) and are forced to return to Punxsutawney for the night. Thus we are introduced to the act of nature, and likely God, that places Phil into his own personal purgatory.

For it is in Punxsutawney, Pennsylvania, that Phil will need to work out his life's meaninglessness. He wakes up in the morning, but it is somehow Groundhog Day again. This is the premise of the movie: Phil is forced to relive Groundhog Day, apparently hundreds of times, until he gets it right. He is the only one who has a memory of the repeated days; for him, today is "again," while for the others, today is "now."

With such a movie, the Christian community is offered up a conversation piece that a number of people in the greater culture seem eager to embrace. Ken Sanes's website, called "Transparency," offers a good deal of discussion of the movie as a seemingly minor comedy that addresses some of our culture's most serious issues (http://www.transparencynow.com/groundhog.htm). In repeating the same day again and again, Phil progresses through a number of stages that Sanes outlines as follows:

- bewilderment
- despair
- risk-taking and treating life as a game with selfish ends
- first breakthrough to intimacy
- generosity and the embracing of life

- shock at, and refusal to accept, death
- acceptance of the circumstances of life and death, and break-through to deep compassion (love)
- being celebrated as a local hero and a second experience of intimacy in which he gets the object of his love

This outline is a fine place to begin a discussion of the film's analysis of our culture's problems in producing lives of meaning, and ultimately an avenue to discussing that culture's proposed solutions.

I teach my college composition students that our culture, in the public sphere, has abandoned conversation for rhetoric. That is, we have moved from the art of listening and responding, to the sport of winning—at whatever cost. Such a discussion is fine for short-term gains, but it is not at all effective for finding long-term solutions to problems. How many minds does *rhetoric* change concerning abortion, global warming, welfare and poverty, racial reconciliation, even the validity of the claims of the gospel?

But real *conversation* takes place under the assumption that content, rather than style, is important, and that both sides have something worth listening to. If we are honest about our political, and even religious, debates, these elements are mainly absent. Certainly, in most cases each speaker comes into a discussion convinced that she or he is correct; conversations in which some-one approaches you believing that he or she has answers and that you do also, are few and far between. But the notion that something can be gained from hearing the other party is a basic aspect of human respect. From these sorts of conversations comes communication, the honing of ideas, interaction.

Groundhog Day is a moment of pause, of vulnerability, where a culture admits that its way of finding meaning in life is not going well. It is eager to converse on the question, "Can the day-to-day aspects of life be meaningful?" Using Sanes's outline of the film, as given above, we'll begin a conversation about this story, and bring in God's stories as well. And finally we'll look at the film's problematic ending.

Stage 1: Bewilderment

Sanes describes the first stage of Phil Connors's reaction to his dilemma as bewilderment. It might be good for us, however, to first define what exactly Connors's dilemma is. Sanes believes that the center of the dilemma is Connors's worldview—that he, to quote one of two regulars Connors meets in a local bowling alley, is a "glass is half-empty kind of guy," and that as the movie progresses, Connors moves to an appreciation of the day-to-day. But at the beginning of the film, Phil Connors clearly believes that seeing the glass as half empty is the only reasonable approach to life. Those people who see life with optimism leave themselves open to disappointment. Connors is not "bewildered" at the beginning of the movie because his point of view changes. Sanes, I believe, means "bewilderment" as Connors's natural reaction to the sudden and unexplained supernatural interruption of his life: someone has changed the rules by which he has chosen to live.

I think that bewilderment is an excellent metaphor, but that the bewilderment Connors experiences here both goes deeper and represents problems of the greater culture (and simply being human) as well. What is at stake with Connors's sense of bewilderment is not just that this day has not gone as expected, or that the rules have changed, but really that life, lived as best he knows how, has not gone as expected. Phil Connors's life has become just as senseless as the lives of the optimists he has long scorned.

Connors's sense of plot for his life is twofold and profoundly American. First, it is safe to say that American culture believes life has a particular plot, and Connors is merely following the culture's track: college, marriage, family, a progressively successful career resulting in a series of successful acquisitions (progressively better homes, cars, clothes, vacations), and a comfortable retirement. The result of all this should be happiness. One would simply want to call this the American dream. Part of Phil Connors's bewilderment as he begins to relive Groundhog Day is that the American dream for Phil has been only partially thought through. He has reached a level of success, but the progression of better jobs has stopped, and with the lack of progression he now faces a lack of satisfaction. What about the hours outside of work?

Second, our culture very much individualizes the American dream along the lines of personal success, but can success be found in the absence of others? Connors finds himself alone. With whom can he share what he has gained? Moreover, when the pace of dream building is suddenly slowed or stalled, Connors has time to assess himself—his behaviors, his personality, his emotional state, his belief system. It seems to me that he is sometimes not sure of who he is confronting, and at other times just not happy with what he sees. But Phil Connors has discovered no directions for what to do if his progress in dream building stops. He is bewildered.

The bewilderment Connors experiences is similar to Solomon's comments in the opening chapters of Ecclesiastes. Solomon does not merely make a list of the things in life that he has found to be without value. The emotion is in the writing. The depth of the cry "Everything is meaningless!" implies that Solomon *expected* these things to bring meaning. He also is bewildered, and the usefulness in comparing the two stories is that Solomon provides an example of what would happen to a person such as Phil Connors in the *best* of circumstances. Solomon is given (and earns) everything, and yet, with the "dream" fully formed, he too is left unsatisfied.

Stage 2: Despair

After the initial shock of his new reality sets in, Phil Connors falls into despair over the reality of his new existence. And here the movie becomes metaphorical, and metaphysical as well. We are laughingly drawn into the realities of Connors's repeated day. For Phil, each day begins with waking up to hear Sonny and Cher on the radio, followed by a recitation on the weather. Each day includes the groundhog ritual (cute at first, perhaps): bitterly cold weather, a moment of being accosted by an old acquaintance from high school who now wants to sell him life insurance, a repeated hometown dose of polka music, and having to shoot the same silly spot for the Pittsburgh television station again and again. But each day ends with the same reality: that tomorrow, in its general outline, will be the same as today. Phil is not living a "greatest hits" reel, but an ordinary existence, over and over.

With this realization comes depression. Phil will never achieve his goals and never get out of the place in which he now resides. He is doomed to monotony and to making meaning where he can; but, again, he does not have experience in finding meaning outside the notion of a grand plan for success. And, eventually, he goes to bed each night with the notion that tomorrow will be the same, despite his initial hopes that maybe the next day will bring a way out.

The movie best shows this in the bowling-alley scene, but I would emphasize a different line in making its point and establishing the metaphor for the movie. Connors, as one can imagine, grows tired of having much the same conversations with the same people, so he begins to get to know some of the locals. One of his choices to pass time, apparently, is bowling. At the bowling alley, where he meets two friends, Phil begins to complain to them about being stuck in a day. Why, Phil asks, did it have to be this day? He would have chosen much more pleasurable days in much nicer places. Can you imagine, he asks, what it is like to wake up each morning and live the same uneventful day over again? His companions look at each other, and one says, "That about sums it up for me."

Stage 3: Risk Taking and Game Playing: Living for Me

How much is this mundane view of day-to-day life at the heart of our culture? Perhaps quite so, for some of the next stages through which Connors travels seem symptomatic of our own culture's tendencies. The risk taking described occurs when Connors begins to toy with the idea that a life with such limiting boundaries must not have consequences, and that meaningless-ness can be treated only by dramatic risk taking. To test this out, he takes his bowling-alley buddies on a joyride, inviting the local police to join in the chase. This includes driving on the train tracks and eventually playing "chicken" with an oncoming train, running into and destroying property for the sake of the chase, and, apparently without thinking through the consequences for his friends, who do not share his purgatory, putting their lives at risk as well. When the chase finally ends, he and his friends are taken to jail, but Connors wakes up the next morning in the same bed-and-breakfast room, listening once again to Sonny and Cher.

Connors's methods of risk taking and conquest are essentially a means of self-stimulation; they are self-medicating devices meant to combat the emptiness of a plotless life. He supplements risk taking with sexual conquest, particularly in attempting to woo Rita, but his attempts are more focused on the conquest itself than with forming a human relationship. He uses his repeated experience of each day to construct a list of her likes and dislikes, her hopes and dreams, as a means of manipulating and attempting to seduce her. Eventually, she sees through his behavior, and his growing desperation results in more and more violent rebuffs.

Solomon, by the way, describes the same reactions: his own attempts to find joy in satisfying his senses and in acquiring turn out to be empty, to the point that even beauty loses its appeal, because he can find only fleeting satisfaction through stimulation—a life made temporarily tolerable by finding something "new." The natural reaction experienced by Connors when his attempts at stimulation fail—for this is all he has been taught—is ultimate despair. At this point in the movie, he repeatedly attempts suicide, the pace of the movie slowing to show two of his attempts; but again, he only awakens the next morning in the same bed to relive the day again. This point in the film is critical, and it would be a place at which I would want to bring Sanes's worldview into conversation. Sanes, rightly so, describes the end of this period as a breakthrough to intimacy. He writes,

> In desperation, he reveals his plight to the female producer and she stays with him (without sex), in his room, through the night. Once again, he wakes up alone in the same day.
>
> But, enriched by this experience of intimacy, and by the fact that someone actually liked him for who he is, he finally figures out a constructive response—he begins to live his life in the day allotted to him, or, rather, he begins to live the life he never lived before. Instead of allowing circumstances to impose themselves on him, he takes control of circumstances, aided by the fact that

he has all the time in the world and the safety of knowing what will happen next.

Sanes's online article on *Groundhog Day* is subtitled, "Breakthrough to the True Self." He believes it is this growing confidence in the true self, and the sense of control that comes with this knowledge, that allows Connors to begin to live a meaningful life. Could it not be true, however, that the truth of what Connors sees, much as what Solomon saw in his wisdom, was not a thoroughly optimistic vision of the self, and certainly not a picture of humans in control of their destinies? The desperation spoken of here is more complicated in the film, and offers an excellent initiation point for discussion.

Connors and his producer are sitting down at breakfast (again), and Connors is eating absurd amounts of food, realizing that what he eats will have no long-term effect on his health. He then begins to explain to Rita that he is God—he knows what will happen all through each day, he knows everyone's secrets and desires. To prove his point, he takes her around the restaurant, explaining the lives of the people there to her and predicting events before they occur. He then tells her that the cameraman will come in soon, and he writes down the words he will say to her, but begs her not to go. He has discovered that his situation has given him a certain omniscience—he has achieved a sense of security, one might say, that our culture equates with success, and he is certainly in control of his world through his knowledge of the day's events, but this omniscience is void of meaning. He finds, interestingly enough, his meaning through weakness: of knowing that he is not God, and of receiving acceptance from Rita because he admits his weaknesses—his humanity. The security one might claim for Phil here is really, I think, an insecurity, a vulnerability. Connors now is driven not by this need for security or control, but, for the first time, by the truth that control is overrated, and by a desire to find on a repeated basis the acceptance and relationship that he eventually finds with Rita.

Sanes breaks down the remainder of the movie into five stages: "generosity and the embracing of life"; "shock at, and refusal to accept, death"; "acceptance of the circumstances of life and death"; a "breakthrough to deep compassion (love)"; and, finally, "being celebrated as a local hero and a second experience of intimacy in which he gets the object of his love." I think, however, that the remainder of the movie is actually a somewhat natural continuation of Connors's turning point and can be divided thus: generosity, based on the taste of acceptance and relationship that he now seeks continually; and embracing life's moments—that is, improving the quality of each hour.

Before his turning point, Connors saw the day-to-day moments of life as monotony, and the pursuit of a "love" (based not on love but on wanting to complete his "conquest" of Rita) as something that was worth patience and continued learning and effort. It is interesting to note that these attitudes are now reversed. He sees the moments of each day as something to invest with patience and continued learning, and, in pursuing love and having compassion for others, he sees that these can be enjoyed only in a day's particular moments, with no promise of reciprocation or continuation. Moreover, the day-to-day investments in appreciating and improving his life are subject to his ability to serve other people.

Connors's investment in improving or enriching himself takes many forms: he takes piano lessons, learns ice sculpting, reads with abandon, and even learns French. He seems to take care of himself physically, mentally, and, to a degree, spiritually. Two aspects of his education are important to note. First, before his transformation, Connors "educated" himself with a purpose of serving only himself. He read French poetry, or learned about Rita's life and desires, as a means of seducing her. After his life reaches its nadir, Connors begins to enjoy what is given to him for what these things are in themselves. There is a sense that he learns to enjoy both French and poetry, mastering a musical instrument or an art form, and knowledge itself. Second, he realizes that life cannot be enjoyed alone. He may have realized some of this before, but he had no long-term interest in the health of others and seemed to see them as still another form of self-directed entertainment. He comes to realize, however, that one's view of others must transcend their potential use to the self, and that the self becomes complete in the service of others.

Seeing life now through the needs of others, Connors begins to pay attention. He uses his knowledge of what each day will bring to "intercept" tragedy. He knows that at a particular time a boy will fall from a tree onto a concrete sidewalk, so he times his day to catch the boy. He is ready to serve when a tire goes flat on a car. He begins to use his knowledge of people's lives to serve them and help them through their own difficulties.

But one of the moist poignant portions of the film concerns Connors's developing relationship with an elderly homeless man. He had passed this man "daily" and had denied him handouts with an expression similar to those we see in ourselves sometimes, as we drive past such men and women at intersections and freeway off-ramps. He then begins to give the old man money—at one point a rather remarkable amount of money. But as the film progresses, Connors begins to see a need for connection to the old man, even though the man is not fully capable of connecting with Connors in return. Connors buys him hot meals, clothes him, attempts to improve his health, but, at the end of the day, despite all he can do, the old man still dies. The end result does not seem to curtail his actions, but the realization of death's control and his desire for meaning and relationship in such a life echo Solomon's assessment:

> There was a man all alone; he had neither son nor brother. There was no end to his toil, yet his eyes were not content with his wealth. "For whom am I toiling," he asked . . . pity the man who falls and has no one to help him up! (Eccles. 4:8, 10)

> The same destiny overtakes all. (Eccles. 9:3)

Connors does not give himself over to hopelessness, however. Choosing the moral imperative of others above self, and allowing the certainty of death to strengthen his valuing of each moment of life, he is seen playing the piano at a wedding reception, accepting the well-wishing of those whom he has served.

The ending of the film is less interesting than this transformation—it seems to fall into formulaic predictability and reaches an unsatisfying conclusion. Connors has reached a point where he can be content in the moment-to-moment of his daily repetitions, and it is then that he is released from his purgatory and allowed to live the next day. At this point, the transformation apparently complete, he abandons the plot he had established for his life and accepts what he has been given: a plot in the details. He courts Rita and decides to stay in Punxsutawney, where his more complete life has been found. Essentially, the end of the film lightens up, and Phil Connors solves his problems by finding true love. One of my students recently described this ending as "cheesy." It backs off the big issues; it makes true love uncomplicated.

The decision to end the film this way may bring Christians into an interesting moment of discussion with the greater culture, and with our own church. Sanes writes the following in summation of the film:

> What is so powerful about *Groundhog Day* is the way it lets us experience what it would be like to make a breakthrough like this in our own lives. The movie shows us a character who is like the worst in ourselves. He is arrogant and sarcastic, absorbed in his own discomforts, without hope, and cut off from other people. Like us, he finds himself in an inexplicable situation, seemingly a plaything of fate. But, unlike us, he gets the luxury of being stuck in the same day until he gets it right. Whereas most of us go semi-automatically through most of our (very similar) days, he is forced to stop and treat each day like a world unto itself, and decide how to use it. In the end, he undergoes a breakthrough to a more authentic self in which intimacy, creativity and compassion come naturally—a self that was trapped inside him and that could only be freed by trapping him. Like many of the heroes of fiction, he can only escape his exile from himself by being exiled in a situation not of his choosing.

The greater culture and the Christian church often find themselves in the unflattering condition of exchanging stereotypes that go something like this: Christians are unself-conscious mouths, telling everyone else what to do, who do not see their own problems (much like the man in Jesus's example of the speck and the beam in the eye); they are moralistic and focused on the end of the world, not the potential quality of life and the realities of human sufferings. Christians may see the greater culture as self-righteous also, dismissing religion and life above the material level, blind to its own shortcomings, trying to make a heaven out of earth without addressing the causes of wrongdoing and human suffering.

But in *Groundhog Day* we have a film that has little to say about God and yet is controlled by a moment of what can only be a divine intervention. And the appeal of the movie, according to Sanes, is that for a moment we can "experience what it would be like to make a breakthrough like this in our own lives." If this desire, given at a moment of pause over a film, expresses a widespread human hope—and I think it does—then the ground for conversation, rather than stereotyping, is set.

But a good amount of our success in such ventures depends on two things that not just the church, but all humans, find frightening and suspect will be ultimately unsuccessful: vulnerability and a commitment to the heart of conversation, which is believing that the other party has something to say that's worth hearing. How are we doing in these areas?

At the end of the second letter to the Church in Corinth, Paul—not usually painted with strokes of humility and vulnerability—gives what to me is one of the most moving testimonies in the New Testament:

> I have worked much harder, been in prison more frequently, been flogged more severely, and been exposed to death again and again. . . . I spent a night and a day in the open sea. . . . I have been in danger from rivers, in danger from bandits, in danger from my own countrymen, in danger from Gentiles; in danger in the city, in danger in the country. . . . I have labored and toiled and have often gone without sleep . . . I have been cold and naked. . . . Therefore I will boast all the more gladly about my weaknesses, so that Christ's power may rest on me. That is why, for Christ's sake, I delight in weaknesses, in insults, in hardships, in persecutions, in difficulties. For when I am weak, then I am strong. (2 Cor. 11:23–27 and 12:9–10)

Do we fall into the cultural trap of planning plots for our lives and becoming lost when these plots don't materialize as planned? Do we grow disappointed when our lives do not seem to match a greatest-hits reel, be it spiritual or materialistic? Or do we turn from these failures, as Solomon and Paul did, with honesty and vulnerability, to seek answers in God and to talk openly about our shared humanity with our neighbors? Life is hard and full of troubles. Life's moments are jewels, especially when joy is found in things we have not made, and in the words of people we do not control. Can we who believe say to those who do not believe, "My life hasn't gone as I had hoped either; but look at these moments of meaning, these jewels, these breakthroughs"?

{ 5 }

Connecting with Christ's Humanity—
Finding Places of Rest in the
Midst of Real Life's Trials

In an earlier chapter, I spoke briefly of our family's move
to the California desert—a kind of exile—after my father's
death. After living in New Jersey in a thoroughly suburban
area, where "nature" was limited to a patch of woods near the
local high school, or a brook that had survived the plans of tract
homes and ran along the edge of my neighbor's backyard, or such
manicured green as a baseball field or a golf course, we moved
to a small desert community where nature was very much still
the dominant force in life, where people seemed to be living at
its pleasure.

The town is named Ridgecrest, which proves that its founder
had a sense of humor of sorts, for it lies in a flat valley between
three ranges of mountains, on neither a ridge nor a crest. It had

originally been near a silver mining town, and had later become a civilian homestead for a nearby military base. While many California desert towns advertise their attractiveness to tired drivers with billboards of swimming pools or golf courses, Ridgecrest's chamber of commerce seemed to have less of a creative bent and admittedly less to work with. The best that they could come up with was a sign near the highway exit that stated, "Welcome to Ridgecrest, Gateway to Death Valley." And, as should be expected in a small community where entertainment for many of its youth is limited (the closest town of any size is sixty miles to the southwest), every year bored high school seniors snuck out in the dead of the night before graduation and removed the word "Valley" from the sign.

My first reaction to Ridgecrest, frankly, was something close to horror. As a child, I had seen similar landscapes on television during the moon landings, or in science-fiction movies (many of which were probably filmed near Ridgecrest): sand and rock, rock and sand—the only signs of Earth, initially, were the small, pathetic, struggling sagebrush that dug their roots deep into the ground and grew despite the constant wind off the mountains.

The desert that encircled Ridgecrest had remained pristine when we had first moved there, and the wildlife that inhabited the valley still viewed the townspeople as squatters. Small sidewinder rattlesnakes wrapped themselves around the cool white out-of-bounds markers on the Navy base's golf course. (I know—why a Navy base in the middle of the desert?) During our first night in our new home our New Jersey-raised housecat cornered a small, green scorpion near some cactus in our backyard and had to be rescued.

But here is what happened: despite the loneliness I experienced from the severity of the move west and the displacement that any child would experience at that age, and despite what initially seemed to be endless sky and sand, I began to experience the landscape.

I had grown up with thunderstorms, but I had done so in the safety and limited skyline of a suburban environment. In the desert, the summer monsoon arrives and thunderclouds explode high into the afternoon sky. At first the clouds develop on the horizon, but then the sky darkens, the wind kicks up dust, and one sees, without buildings to obstruct the view, the power of a storm. Lightning connects sky to ground, rain and wind sweep across miles of open land and crash into the buildings and trees of the town's paltry resistance. And the desert on a summer night presents a different sort of transformation. When the sun sets, the temperature drops quickly, and the lack of humidity can make the wind on even an eighty-degree evening feel cool against your skin. At a nearby college, on a hill just outside of town, was a place one could access by a short drive and, sitting in the darkness of the evening, see the lights of the town below and the endless sweep of stars above. The sky was not just a canopy of lights, but a three-dimensional valley of shooting stars, the Milky Way in all its complexity and richness, and a range of star colors and intensities. In such a landscape, even in the midst of a sense of exile, my problems and my very being became smaller, and the sense of the creation and the Creator lived in ways I had never known.

So nature became, and still is, my solace. In the midst of un-settling times, I seek out wild places—the more empty the bet-ter—to reconnect with God and a sense of his power. I leave the "white noise" and interference of everyday life to be alone with the Creator. Two novels strike me as understanding the healing role of the creation in the midst of the trials of real life; both are departures of sorts. The novels are Anne Rice's *Christ the Lord: Out of Egypt* and Leif Enger's *Peace Like a River*.

Finding Rest in God's Landscape

Christ the Lord: Out of Egypt is the result of years of searching and a decision. Anne Rice describes her unexpected reencounter with God (she was raised Roman Catholic and departed from the faith as a young adult) as taking place in the late 1990s as she studied the history of the Jewish people—a history of survival that made little historical sense outside of the existence of a God. From there, Rice went on to try to understand Jesus and the emergence of Christianity. She writes,

> I wanted to write the life of Jesus Christ. I had known that years ago. But now I was ready. I was ready to do violence to my career. I wanted to write the book in the first person. Nothing else mattered . . . I consecrated myself and my work to Christ. (309)

She describes the intellectual milieu from which she began to work—intellectually "fashionable notions" about Jesus—and the shock she encountered when she decided to begin her true historical research (as she has researched the backdrop for all of her novels): the size of the academic field was, she writes, "virtually without end."

From 2002, after the sudden death of her husband of forty-one years, until 2005, Rice studied the New Testament period, trying to piece together a legitimate cultural backdrop for her novel and working her way through a wide range of biblical criticism, beginning with the skeptics; she did this with considerable trepidation, fearing that her refound faith, still in its infancy, would be shaken by their arguments. To her surprise, she found much of the skeptical scholarship to be unscholarly; it contained assumptions and emotions she would not expect to encounter in the study of other academic subjects. The author's note at the end of her novel describes this process in the detail it deserves.

What Rice settled on was the challenge of writing about "the Jesus of the Gospels"—the results of her quest require a moment of explanation. *Christ the Lord* is not a narrative retelling of the Gospels themselves, but a historical fiction (a novel that attempts to realistically recreate the cultural background of its characters) that endeavors to capture a few years of Jesus in his childhood, about which little is known, and to be true to the Jesus of the Gospels whom the child would grow up to become. In doing so, Rice relies on her rich cultural research, on two or three works in particular that try to recreate everyday life in first-century Egypt and Israel, and on what she refers to as legends (such as the Gospel of Thomas) for a couple of the novel's early instances. But Rice's challenge in this novel, the tone of which is unassuming despite highly ambitious subject matter, is to capture a moment in the life of Jesus that Christians typically do not consider, but to which, I believe, we are quite capable of connecting.

One of Rice's characters, Cleopas (an uncle of Jesus), outlines the problem of the novel. While Joseph and Mary are often reticent concerning the young boy's questions, Cleopas attempts to help a seven-year-old Jesus piece together the mystery of his birth. Rice's Jesus at this stage of his life has an intuitive sense of who he is, but nothing that can yet be verbalized or fully understood. Among his questions are the incidents in his life about which he has only heard rumors and whispers: the details of his birth in Bethlehem, the visit of the Magi and Herod's subsequent rage, the annunciation of the angel to Mary in proclaiming the origins of the child she will bear, the relationship of Joseph and his mother. The young Jesus notices a physical aversion between them. Joseph's manner in discussing information about Jesus's birth is quiet, reserved—something the child mistakes for doubt. Cleopas clarifies for Jesus:

"Turn it around . . . [Joseph] never touches [Mary, Jesus's mother] because he does believe. Don't you see? How could he touch her after such a thing?" He smiled, and then he laughed in that low laugh of his, but no one else heard it. "And you?" he went on. "Must you grow up before you fulfill the prophecies? Yes, you must. And must you be a child before you are a man? Yes. How else? . . . Don't you see, that's what confounds them all! You must grow up like any other child!" (47)

In order to help us connect with Jesus, to understand the applicability of his human existence to our own lives and to our own struggles in discerning God's plot in this world, Anne Rice presents the Son of God as a frighteningly vulnerable child, growing up like any other child—like any of us—in a world of violence, senselessness, and unanswered questions.

Imagine for a moment, as Anne Rice does, the world in which this Jesus, who must be a child before he is a man, grows up. Rice does not portray him as merely human—and that adds to the child's mystery. He hears whispers among his family that his birth was foretold, and he hears of strange and sometimes awful events—the appearance of the angels, Herod's decision to slaughter young children in Bethlehem in an attempt, as he often did, to eliminate any who could claim his throne. This Jesus lives his early life in a Jewish community in Alexandria, trained in his father's profession of carpentry, and then, still a young child, he returns to Israel with his family upon the death of Herod.

But Israel itself, despite and because of the tyrant's death, is far from well. The country falls into violence and chaos as Herod's son tries to establish his throne and as those elements of Jewish society long repressed by his father's tyranny violently try to claim the country for themselves. The young Jesus witnesses slaughter in the very temple in Jerusalem at the Passover and is in constant danger from thieves and uprisings as he and his family make their way through an unsettled country to his home in Nazareth. As the lid of Herod's tyranny is taken off the country, years of repressed lawlessness explodes, leaving few places safe for a child who is leaving the only home he has known for a family home he has never experienced.

The novel is full of these scenes of violence—prescient glimpses that further the mystery for a Jesus whose perceptions for now outweigh his reason. As the party approaches Nazareth, word of a rebellion led by one Judas bar Ezekias, who has set up court in a nearby town, Sphoris, reaches them. But the occupying Roman forces stop the rebellion by crucifying the innocent with the guilty on the town's outskirts.

Even in Nazareth, young Jesus is subject to trouble: the Rabbis of the local synagogue hesitate to give him access to the house of prayer because of questions concerning his birth—questions that again the seven-year-old Jesus intuits but does not yet fully understand. Rice writes,

> But a tall man stood to the left, a man with a very long soft-looking black and gray beard and so much beard on his upper lip that I could hardly see his mouth. His eyes were dark, and his hair was long, to his shoulders, only a little gray, under his prayer shawl.
>
> He put his hand in front of me.
>
> The man spoke in a very soft voice, looking at me as he did, but his words were for others.
>
> "I know James, yes, and Silas and Levi, I remember them, but this one? Who is this one . . ."
>
> It was very quiet.
>
> I saw that everyone in the synagogue was looking at us. I didn't like it. I was beginning to be scared of it. (161)

So the details of Jesus's birth and thus his right to be accepted into his religious community are questioned; he is taken from his home; his family has secrets about which they will not speak; even the country itself has fallen into chaos. And through all of this he must be a child before he can be a man. I think that part of the power of Rice's book is found in the fact that we, in a world of divine plots and human danger, are still much like children. Our vision is limited, and we are vulnerable to all of life's dangers and inevitabilities. We are in exile—away from the world as it should be.

The seven-year-old Jesus whom Rice invents finds solace from these childhood fears in places that will match where the Jesus of the Gospels finds peace—and also often the places in which he experiences power. Jesus takes his disciples with him out of the crowds into a small town, Bethsaida, but the crowds find him there, and it is there that he feeds the multitudes. He takes three of his disciples with him into the wilderness of a mountain to pray, and it is there that they experience Jesus's transfiguration, where "the appearance of [Jesus's] face changed, and his clothes became as bright as a flash of lightning" (Luke 9:28–29). He retreats into a garden on the Mount of Olives outside of Jerusalem the night before his death and there wrestles with his Father, finally submitting to his will.

> Sometimes the issue is not that life lacks a plot; instead, the details of life—its stresses, tragedies, day-to-day grinds, and detours—cause us to lose our plots.

Rice shows the child Jesus seeking out nature and finding the divine there in ways that anticipate the Gospel accounts. Jesus narrates:

> I lay down on the grass, and felt the wildflowers with my open hand. . . . I loved this place. I knew love of it, love of thick forests

going up the slopes with the cypress and the sycamore, and the myrtle trees as Joseph taught me the names of them.

I prayed in my heart. "Father in Heaven, I thank you for this." (200, 211)

These respites alone in the creation give Jesus, caught in the limitations of his childhood and the violence of his world, time to regain perspective. This retreat into the country is a device used in literature—but it is used because of its effectiveness in real life. In my introduction to literature courses, I explain the retreat from the city (and the troubling circumstances it usually embodies for a literary character in crisis) into the country (apart from the "footprint" of humankind) is not a means of changing the realities of one's life, but as a way of regaining perspective on what those realities mean in light of all that one still has. If life in Chicago is falling apart, then three days in rural Wisconsin—where one is forced to slow down, and listen to the quiet, and reacquaint one's senses with the realities of nature that are paved over by the city and its troubles—reminds one of all that has not fallen apart in the world and in one's life. One returns from the country with the same circumstances, but with a changed mind-set that is able to address those circumstances differently. This is the primary purpose of spiritual retreat—not to transfer one's busy schedule to a programmed weekend of more busyness, but to tune out the noise of life and retune into the larger music of the creation.

Sometimes the issue is not that life lacks a plot; instead, the details of life—its stresses, tragedies, day-to-day grinds, and detours—cause us to lose our plots. We need a quiet place, apart from the objects and troubles of humankind's making, to hear God's voice. We need a retreat. The fact that Jesus himself, our perfect model for human life, needed these places of retreat leaves us with little excuse for not seeking them out.

Christ the Lord ends with one of these quiet places, and the child Jesus pieces together both the secrets of his birth and the much more difficult meaning of his life:

> I went outside. It was getting dark. I walked through the street and out to the hillside and up to where the grass was soft and undisturbed. This was my favorite place, just short of the grove of trees near which I loved so to rest.
>
> I looked up at the first few stars coming through the twilight.
>
> Born to die, I thought. Yes, born to die. Why else would I be born of a woman? Why else would I be flesh and blood if it wasn't to die? . . .
>
> A quiet fell over me, just when I thought my heart would burst.
>
> The answer came as if from the earth itself, as if from the stars, and the soft grass, and the nearby trees, and the purring of the evening.
>
> . . . I was sent here to be alive. To breathe and sweat and thirst and sometimes cry.
>
> And everything that happened to me, everything both great and small, was something I had to learn! There was room for it in the infinite mind of the Lord and I had to seek the lesson in it, no matter how hard it was to find.
>
> . . . It seemed the whole world was holding me. Why had I ever thought I was alone? I was in the embrace of the earth, of those who loved me no matter what they thought or understood, of the very stars.
>
> "Father," I said, "I am your child." (300–301)

That, as Rice's Jesus states, we are given life to "breathe and sweat and thirst and sometimes cry" does not mean that life is plotless or meaningless; it means that these elements are simply part of human existence—the same experiences of richness and work and suffering that Jesus himself came to share with us. He understands us because he chose to become like us. Our comfort is that he never lost his plot, despite all he endured.

Finding Rest in God's Moments of Interruption

The relationship that the child Jesus finds to his Father in nature, in which he takes comfort that he will be able to learn life's lessons, is experienced in a human father-and-son relationship in Leif Enger's 2001 novel, *Peace Like a River*. The novel's landscapes are often bleak—those of the Great Plains badlands in winter—but the warmth experienced by the novel's protagonist finds its base in family, even when the circumstances of the family seem far from stable. But this particular relationship offers more: it offers a glimpse into the miraculous—those moments when God in his grace interrupts the natural order. Enger writes, in the novel's first chapter,

> Let me say something about that word: miracle. For too long it's been used to characterize things or events that, though pleasant, are entirely normal. Peeping chicks at Easter time, spring generally, a clear sunrise after an overcast week—a miracle, people say, as if they've been educated from greeting cards. I'm sorry, but nope. Such things are worth our notice every day of the week, but to call them miracles evaporates the strength of the word.
>
> Real miracles bother people, like strange sudden pains unknown in medical literature. It's true: They rebut every rule all we good citizens take comfort in. Lazarus obeying orders and climbing up out of the grave—now there's a miracle, and you can bet it upset a lot of folks who were standing around at the time. When a person dies, the earth is generally unwilling to cough him back up. A miracle contradicts the will of the earth.
>
> . . . People fear miracles because they fear being changed—though ignoring them will change you also. [My sister] said an-

other thing, too, and it rang in me like a bell: No miracle happens without a witness. Someone to declare, Here's what I saw. Here's how it went. Make of it what you will. (3)

According to Enger, miracles are disbelieved because believing them would require a person and their point of view to change. In a 2004 interview with *Writers and Books,* Enger affirms this by reminding the interviewer that "you cannot compel belief"; instead, you can only quietly tell the story. The listener then receives it, or chooses not to receive it. So, finally, the "choice" of not changing is a false choice. In either receiving or rejecting, one is changed; in rejecting, specifically, the irony is that a person's desire to hold on to reality causes reality itself, if the miracle is true, to be modified in order to fit the disbeliever's worldview. The miracle is scaled down because we can't take the implications of real miracles.

The miracles in Enger's book are both limited and various, but each works as a signpost in the life of the narrator, Reuben Land, of God's presence in his life when life seems to have spun out of control. They are markers of meaning. The first marks Reuben's birth: the infant boy's lungs are "swampy" at birth, and the doctor cannot get the newborn boy to breathe. Reuben slowly turns into a child of gray clay as twelve minutes pass without respiration. Jeremiah Land, his father, who is pacing outside the hospital during the delivery, gets a sense from God that his child is in trouble and rushes into the delivery room, where he has to physically "convince" the doctor to let him near his son. Jeremiah then states, "in a normal voice, 'Reuben Land, in the name of the living God I am telling you to breathe.'" Enger finishes the story quietly, with a humor that disarms the reader and allows him or her to digest the miracle without an immediate compulsion to believe it:

. . . the doctor turned out wrong about the brain damage. I'm happy to say none surfaced until I entered tenth grade and signed up for Plane Geometry; but since I still feed myself and grind out a sentence in English, you won't hear me complain. (5)

The next miracle involves Jeremiah's prayer as he paces on a flatbed. Eyes closed, he walks over the edge and, with only young Reuben as a witness (and Jeremiah himself oblivious), does not fall. In the next, Jeremiah interrupts the attempted rape of his older son's girlfriend in the high school boys' locker room (Jeremiah is the school janitor); the girl later describes Jeremiah's presence in the darkened room as "luminous of itself, glowing and serene, the way you'd suppose an angel's would be . . ." (24). This incident leads to an "escalation" of hostilities that will lead to the novel's tragic, driving moment. Reuben then witnesses a Pentecostal service in which his dad is touched by the Holy Spirit, and Reuben himself, touched by the hand of the reverend, feels something like an electric shock surging through his body and a loosening of his lungs.

The miracles continue: a small pot of soup that ends up feeding a hungry traveling salesman and the family, replenishing itself; the returning to new of an old leather saddle bought for Reuben's sister; the story of a tornado that caught Jeremiah Land, in the early years of his marriage, and "baptized" him into a new life that saw him forsake his ambitious plans—as a result, his wife leaves him; and the miraculous healing of Jeremiah Land's hated boss, who falsely accuses Land of drunkenness.

Now, as you read through this abbreviated list of reported miracles, chances are that some items evoke a reaction in you close to skepticism. You might think of logical explanations for the events; you might, perhaps, even dismiss the notion of the miraculous happening in such an obvious way. Perhaps your definition of *miracle* is closer to the one that Reuben waves off at the beginning of the novel. As I mentioned in a previous chapter, in the Gospel accounts, reactions to Jesus's miracles are often divided, and this sort of reaction seem human. Some dismiss the voice of God during Jesus's baptism as thunder. For others, past miracles are never enough—just one more, please, the crowds and the religious leaders often ask of Jesus. But God seems to insist that these events, these miracles, are not only to be believed, but to be held tight, again as markers of his presence in and interruption of the seeming plotlessness of our world. When a miracle has happened, typically a major life circumstance has changed. But what happens if we walk away from a situation in which the circumstance has changed, but we have not? Life returns to "normal" and we are able to put aside the implications of God's work just by the passing of time.

The Hebrews, upon coming into their own land, are consistently asked to look back upon the miracles that God performed in bringing them out of Egypt and in feeding them when they were hungry and wandering in the desert. They do this so that, when they have planted fields and built houses—once the crisis has passed—they do not forget the Lord their God who brought them out of Egypt. Mary, the mother of Jesus, counts the miracles surrounding Jesus's birth as reminders of the Lord her God who interrupted life. She "treasured up all these things and pondered them in her heart" (Luke 2:19). The apostles' ministries are filled with these miraculous moments, and I can picture them, through their trials, waiting in jail cells, hanging on to what God did.

I bring this to your attention because of what such moments, and the reactions to them, mean to us today. As I wrote before, when my son was diagnosed with autism around his third birthday, the diagnosis was not ambiguous, and it was made by doctors at a leading hospital who saw this condition all the time. Six of twelve symptoms listed for autism in the *Diagnostic and Statistical Manual of Mental Disorders* are needed for a diagnosis; my son satisfied ten of the twelve. Yet, as he improved and repeatedly defied the expectation of his diagnosis, we experienced a range of reactions, most of them against something miraculous taking place: the original diagnosis was wrong; the progress he was experiencing wasn't real; the parents' hard work had paid off. Now take these reactions and apply them to a biblical miracle, say, that of the raising of Lazarus: the diagnosis was wrong (Lazarus wasn't really dead); the progress wasn't real (the Lazarus that people now saw sitting at the dinner table really was still dead, or could revert at any second); Jesus should be congratulated on his very human hard work in restoring to life a decomposing corpse. These are human reactions to the miraculous; they're present in our reactions to the instances of the miraculous we encounter in our lives, and, interestingly enough, they are common types of reactions to the Christian proclamation of the reality of the resurrection of Jesus from the dead.

But my wife and I have chosen to hold the evidence of our son's recovery in our hearts. There are still signs of a condition, especially if you know what to look for (much as Jacob's limp in the Old Testament story was a sign of his previous struggle to believe, and much as the effects of the life prior to conversion that Anne Lamott describes in her autobiography are still present in her Christian life). But I have experienced things regarding my son, some of them too personal to share in a book, that I have chosen to hold in my heart, markers of God's presence in my life and his decision to interrupt my son's diagnosis. A prognosis, after all, is merely a prediction of how a disease will turn out if it is not interrupted. But God interrupts our lives.

Perhaps the most difficult thing about witnessing miracles is not experiencing the ones we hope for most. Jeremiah Land would gladly exchange his life for that of his troubled older son. Reuben wonders why, given all of the miracles he sees accomplished through his father who dearly loves him, his own lungs cannot be healed. One answer to this dilemma has to do with another complexity of plot and plotlessness. The Old Testament scriptures put it simply: God's ways are not our ways.

Our skeptical natures react to such a statement by seeing it as an "asterisk" in the nature of the miraculous—an out clause that allows us to maintain an intellectual belief without being affected by the facts. I want to state explicitly that this is not the case. Some Christians have, perhaps, been too quick to utter "it must not be God's will" as a way of protecting themselves against the apparent lack of the miraculous in a given situation. But if we are to believe in a God who has the power to interrupt the natural order, it makes sense also to believe that such a God may be a bit beyond us, and that our comparatively limited perspectives might not serve up the best answers to the problems we confront. That is to say: we count on answers themselves, but not on receiving the answers in the manner we necessarily expect.

> Perhaps the most difficult thing about witnessing miracles is not experiencing the ones we hope for most.

In these situations comes a call for difficult faith. Please understand, there is plenty of biblical evidence for this sort of faith being the norm in the life of the believer. We're given a glimpse of it through the biblical explication provided by Anne Rice's novel. Mary, having believed the angel's proclamation that the child in her womb was the seed of God himself, having endured the scorn of her town's neighbors and religious leaders, having endured the first instinct of her husband (upon receiving the news, to divorce her quietly), arrives far from home in Bethlehem, the birth imminent, only to find that the inn is full and that she will have to have the child in a cave. She is devastated: I have played by the rules, I have excelled in the kind of faith for which God rewards people, and the child is to be born in a cave. And then, of course, the shepherds come, telling of angels.

> But sometimes the miracle comes, or becomes visible, after our expectations of what should happen and how it should happen are lost.

So it goes: even despite our desire to believe, our decision to hold on to our notion of how a miracle should unfold leaves us in the unfortunate position of not expecting miracles. That is, if life doesn't turn out the way we would like, one understandable human reaction is to give up hope. But sometimes the miracle comes, or becomes visible, after our expectations of what should happen and how it should happen are lost.

Here is a final example from *Peace Like a River*. Reuben Land came to a low point in his life just before the conclusion of the novel. Reuben has lied to protect his brother and, in doing so, has injured his family and others enlisted in the search for him. Thus, his own failure eclipses his faith, despite the litany of miracles he has held close in his heart. Reuben narrates:

> I don't like to admit it. Shouldn't that be the last thing you release: the hope that the Lord God, touched in His heart by your particular impasse among all others, will reach down and do that work none else can accomplish—straighten the twist, clear the oozing sore, open the lungs? Who knew better than I that such holy stuff occurs? Who had more reason to hope? (292)

The answer that Reuben receives is the most miraculous in the book, something he would not have chosen, and thus an event requiring the most faith to the reader of this story.

Reuben Land receives the healing of his lungs, but only through the ultimate sacrifice of his father. Both are near death at the end of the novel, and Reuben, in the country between this life and the next, has a vision of his father alongside him in a place that draws him. Reuben's father sends him home, though, lungs healed, guaranteeing his young son that they will meet again in a place where they will both be healed. Reuben, then, both gains and loses the desire of his heart. And this sometimes is how our lives go: we lose what we love and find what we had always hoped for. Who of all the disciples would have ever accepted the notion that their Jesus would be lost to them—that he would have to die—as good news? Who among them could have ever imagined what they would gain—salvation and forgiveness and meaning—through his death and triumph over the grave?

This sort of miracle—the kind requiring this hard faith—may be the one best kept close to our own hearts as we sort out our plotlessness and wait for the revealing of God's plot in our lives. Like Mary, we may come to what seems to be the end of a journey only to find a cold, empty cave on a winter's night. But then the angels sing.

{ 6 }

Connecting with God's Plot—
Finding Meaning in Real Life's
Unexpected Turns

After I had been a Christian about two years, I decided to move myself from the church where I had first heard the gospel as an adult—a church of about 10,000 attendees where it was challenging to get to know people—to a small church, not far from my home. The smaller church had its idiosyncrasies, but in it I learned the Bible and became part of a small group of believers my age: it was a time of honesty and growth. One of the emphases of the new church—and one of the burdens, I think, of the senior pastor—was the desire for all the members of the congregation to do missionary work overseas, and this burden was not expressed in a particularly gentle way. Missionaries regularly would be invited to the Sunday morning and evening services in order to report on their activities abroad and, it seemed, to pronounce the same message: do NOT resist the will of God in these matters. They recounted their own experiences as young men or women of saying things like, "Whatever you do, God, please do not make me a missionary," and then, next thing they knew, they were at the front of the church signing up to go to Papua New Guinea. I listened to these testimonies under duress. I did not want to go to a dangerous, foreign place to suffer a spare, lonely life among resistant peoples. And so, I spent those times in church in a combined state of tension and guilt.

Years later, after I had married, had two children, and was completing a PhD in English literature, my wife and I made a decision as we entered the job search: we would go where we felt called to go—although I imagine we added in our own minds, "within reason." Our understanding of God's will and leading had changed since my time of first listening to the missionaries: God might send you to places that you would never choose on your own, but in some way these places would fit you. You would discover why you, and not someone else, were sent there. And, we had also realized that "mission work" could take place in your own neighborhood.

The job search led us to North Park College (now University) in Chicago—irony of ironies. I was the only child in my family *not* born in Chicago. My father grew up in Hyde Park, my mother in the central south side of the city. And now, I was the only family member who would be living there. I remember how odd Chicago looked to us: lines of brick houses, the likes of which we never had seen in earthquake-prone southern California; old, narrow side streets that must not have been built for cars; and flatness, endless flatness—a café near our house was called the Hilltop Cafe, and it took us literally years to notice the slow, paltry incline that constituted the "hill." We lived on the second floor of a beautiful old brick two-flat just a short block north of campus with a bay of windows at the front and one side of the living room. One evening shortly after we had moved to Chicago, we were there in the house together, admiring the windows, when we noticed a sudden collection of police cars on our street. As we leaned into the windows to get a better view, men in black uniforms and flak jackets raced out of the cars and surrounded a small bungalow just two houses up from us, guns drawn. And, out one of the windows of the bungalow, we saw another gun—that of the owner—emerge. We then realized that being next to the beautiful bay windows was probably not a good idea.

Later that night, it hit me. I had pleaded with God ten years ago to not send me to a foreign, dangerous place, and he had sent us to Chicago! But North Park was a fit for me, and Terry found her vocation in Chicago.

There are, of course, more serious turns in life where the unexpected becomes the reality. And, from the statistics on divorce, our society does not do well with the unexpected. When our son was diagnosed with autism, about six months after our move, the stress of the situation translated quickly into sink or swim. Marriages often do not survive a tragedy involving a child—the couple either quickly grows together or fractures and moves apart. But even less devastating changes apparently end marriages in our culture: financial challenges, career changes, anything that departs from a preconceived, and usually naive, notion of what marriage should be. We live in a society of successes and prosperity lined with stress fractures. As pressures pull our lives in different directions, the fractures begin to show. We can let go of some of the conflicting causes, but sometimes we don't want to let go, and sometimes repairing the fractures leaves marks on the original—signs of stress and trouble and brokenness that we would rather not have others see. Apparently, we would rather have the whole thing blow apart than apply the glue.

Is it a particular danger in the believer's journey with God to at some point confuse God's desires for our own? Do we come to a point where, originally intent on finding and following God's plot for our lives, we assimilate his plot so that it finally becomes only a cosmetically Christian version of our own desires? Twelve years after our move to Chicago, my wife and I, as she finished medical school, were being moved again by God's plot, and it became clear to us that my time at North Park was coming to an end. I shared a number of conversations with a colleague there, who found himself leaving at the same time. He had come to the university with a strong sense of call, but as time went on, he became less and less happy there: a number of events that seemed to be in God's plans for him did not transpire, and he found himself at a loss, feeling alienated from the direction his life was taking. At the end of our tenure there, he told me that he was coming to terms with the notion that praying "Thy will be done" does not necessarily mean "My will be done."

Plot is not easy to assess when one is in the middle of the action. Charles Dickens, one of the masters of the novel, is famous for his complicated and minutely detailed plots. His protagonists, however, almost never discern the correct direction of the plot they find themselves in. Pip in *Great Expectations* so obsesses over his own notion of what life "should be" that the truth, when revealed, turns his very world upside down. How do we divide God's plot for us from our own desires? And what do we do with the circumstances in which we find ourselves, in which

> We live in a society of successes and prosperity lined with stress fractures. As pressures pull our lives in different directions, the fractures begin to show.

little plot seems visible? In order to answer these questions, we'll look at two stories: that of Joseph in the Old Testament, and a film by Danish director Gabriel Axel, *Babette's Feast*. Many of the answers to separating God's plot from our own seem to rest in our focus: not "What does God want for me?" but "What does God want for others?"

> Plot is not easy to assess when one is in the middle of the action.

Dreams and Realities

Joseph, the son of Jacob, was the youngest child in a large family. Like many youngest children, he was the apple of his father's eye, and this fact was not lost on his brothers. To make matters worse, from what we can tell, Joseph either believed that he was better than his brothers, or enjoyed lording the parental favoritism over them. In any case, the results were not a peaceful sibling dynamic.

In Genesis, chapter 37, we are told of two offenses that epitomized the problem. Joseph comes from a family of shepherds, and one day he goes to check on his brothers' work and brings back a bad report to his father. This is a simple incident, but one can only imagine the disdain it won him. The text goes as far as to say that his brothers "hated him and could not speak a kind word to him" (Gen. 37:4). To make matters worse, Joseph was a young man who had dreams—literally. In those days and in that culture, dreams were seen as a vehicle for prophetic messages from God, and the substance of the messages that Joseph received did not please his family:

> Joseph had a dream, and when he told it to his brothers, they hated him all the more. He said to them, "Listen to this dream

I had: We were binding sheaves of grain out in the field when suddenly my sheaf rose and stood upright, while your sheaves gathered around mine and bowed down to it."

His brothers said to him, "Do you intend to reign over us? Will you actually rule us?" And they hated him all the more because of his dream and what he had said.

Then he had another dream, and he told it to his brothers. "Listen," he said, "I had another dream, and this time the sun and moon and eleven stars were bowing down to me."

When he told his father as well as his brothers, his father rebuked him and said, "What is this dream you had? Will your mother and I and your brothers actually come and bow down to the ground before you?" His brothers were jealous of him, but his father kept the matter in mind. (Gen. 37:5–11)

So when shortly after this Joseph went to check up on his brothers' work again, they had had enough. The more violent among them plotted his death; the more cautious just decided to throw him into a large cistern from which he could not escape and let whatever would happen, happen. Finally, some of the brothers desired to get something out of the deal, so they sold Joseph to a caravan on its way to Egypt. Joseph's oldest brother, Reuben, realizing that he would be held responsible by his father for Joseph's fate, was appalled at what had transpired in his absence, but he only worked to cover up his brothers' misdeeds by tearing the robe Joseph had left behind and by smearing it with blood so that his father would believe that his favorite son had been torn apart by wild beasts.

Joseph, meanwhile, arrived in Egypt and was sold to Potiphar, the captain of Pharaoh's guard. A pattern ensued: no matter what circumstances Joseph found himself in—and they were rarely desirable—God blessed him, and then all went seemingly awry. Potiphar found the boy to be talented and so put him in charge of his household. Unfortunately, Potiphar's wife found Joseph attractive, tried to seduce him, and, angered by his refusal, accused him of rape. Joseph was sent to prison, where the warden, seeing his talents as well, placed him in charge of the other prisoners. Joseph there was given the opportunity to interpret dreams. God gave him the correct interpretation for a dream of a servant of Pharaoh who had fallen out of favor, and asked the man to remember him when, as the dream foretold, he would be released and restored to his former place in the court. But the man, likely delighted at his release, forgot, and Joseph languished in prison.

What could Joseph have made of God's plot for his life? He went from a favorite son to a captive in a foreign land. To complicate the situation, it was evident to Joseph that God had not forgotten him—he enjoyed supernatural favor and intervention, but the situation seemed only to get worse. Joseph apparently believed that he would become the head of his family, and so acknowledged by his brothers and parents, but he found only rebuke there. And what of the grandeur of the second dream, in which the very sun, moon, and stars bow down to him? Could this sort of honor not even transcend the confines of his family? But Joseph, now in the prime of his life, seemed to have been forgotten by God as he languished in the dungeon.

As Joseph attempted to reconcile what he believed was God's plot for his life (as revealed in his dreams and by his father's favor) with his current realities, so I as a reader sometimes fall into the same pattern of error. Certainly, I may think, this is just a temporary setback and, knowing the whole story as I may, I await the moment for Joseph to be lifted by God to his long-awaited place of honor. But the plot into which Joseph's life continues proves complicated: finding God's plot is not just a restoration of

Joseph's previous desires. As my friend said, "Thy will be done" does not mean "My will be done."

The text tells us that Joseph remained in prison for two years. At the end of this period, Pharaoh had a series of nightmares in which he witnessed healthy grain swallowed up by grain that was thin and scorched, and in which healthy cattle were devoured by emaciated cows that came up from the great Nile River. Pharaoh must have experienced a profound sense of foreboding, for he demanded interpretations from his court, but found no answers to these dreams from his magicians and his wise men. The servant who had been restored to favor two years before then remembered his forgotten promise to Joseph, and informed Pharaoh that there was a young man he knew who could interpret dreams. Joseph was released and, citing God as his source for interpretation, told Pharaoh that his two dreams were one and the same: Egypt would experience seven years of plenty, but the seven years that were to follow those years would contain a famine so severe that the memory of the seven good years would be wiped from memory. Joseph recommended that Pharaoh immediately set up a system in which a panel of commissioners and a ruler over them would reserve grain from the plentiful years to get Egypt through the famine.

We might think here that Joseph has finally been honored according to his dreams, or that he is attempting to at least grasp an opportunity to regain his plot as he sees it, but the situation he enters is not easy. Imagine the political realities of a ruler coming to others in his government and declaring his intent to reserve a large amount of a budget surplus for a deficit he *thinks* will be coming seven years from now. I can recall very few examples in which a political body tended to act responsibly with surpluses, or even believed that those surpluses would not last forever. When Pharaoh placed Joseph in charge of the agency that would collect goods from the people, he was no fool: who would want to head such a commission? Moreover, imagine the local reaction when this charge was given to a foreigner, an unknown. I believe that Pharaoh was hedging his bets.

However, the famine did indeed come, and the job Joseph was given became worse than perhaps he expected. There was food in Egypt due to Joseph's thrift, but he instructed the grain he had stored to be sold to the people of Egypt, and in the end the people had given their money, livestock, land, and even themselves to Pharaoh, so that Pharaoh ended up not just the ruler, but the owner of all of Egypt. (See Gen. 47:13–26.) Joseph's success in Egypt was bittersweet, as was evidenced by the naming of his children born to him there. Manasseh, his firstborn, means "to forget." He named his second Ephraim, "twice fruitful," because "God has made me fruitful in the land of my suffering."

As God's plot for Joseph's life unfolds, we do not see him returning in glory to his family or to his homeland; instead, the famine drives his father to send Joseph's brothers to look for food in Egypt. There they encounter their younger brother, unlooked-for and unrecognizable as Pharaoh's regent, and after a long episode in which Joseph seeks to even the score, they do bow down to him. But Joseph does not deal out justice; he offers them and his father mercy. He brings them into a good part of the land to live, and tries to comfort them regarding their crimes against him with these words:

> And now, do not be distressed and do not be angry with yourselves for selling me here, because it was to save lives that God sent me ahead of you. (Gen. 45:5)

At this point Joseph sees *some* of the big picture, of God's plans for him apart from his own notion of those plans. Life has been hard for Joseph, and what happened to him was meant for evil by his brothers. But God was able to transform those evils into a different sort of good for Joseph—something both bittersweet and victorious, something that allowed him to act in ways he had never "dreamed," and in ways that benefited so many more than just himself. We are given just a hint here that he comes to see life not just as something that is about his own goals. The goodness he internalizes comes through misdirection, through unexpected turns, and in a form that transcends his own limited notion of success. It is goodness with a cost, but goodness in larger terms. As we read the story, perhaps we concentrate on Joseph's position in the government or his power over those who have done him wrong, but the years in exile have wrenched personal changes in Joseph. He is able to forgive those who tore his very life from him, and he is able to point to God's plot instead of his own.

Life as a Feast in the Wilderness

Some of our culture's moments of true pause and introspection come in the movie theater, or even in a darkened living room in front of a television and DVD player, where for a few hours the world is shut out and we take stock of our values and hopes. We pause from our own concerns and allow ourselves to become absorbed in the story of another. And, as so often happens, as we gain even that small distance from ourselves, the problems and solutions we see in the lives of the film's characters shed unexpected light on our own concerns. We can come to see the world in entirely new ways.

The film *Babette's Feast* is an adaptation of Karen Blixsen's (writing under the pseudonym of Isak Dinesen) story, taken from a collection of her stories, *Anecdotes of Destiny*. Blixen, who is more famous for her tale *Out of Africa,* was dying when she wrote the story, coming to terms with a career that had not turned out as expected. The film, written and directed by Danish director Gabriel Axel and set in Denmark, won the Academy Award for Best Foreign Language Film in 1987, twenty-five years after Blixen's death.

The story concerns the arrival of a French exile, Babette, in a small, isolated Jutland religious community; the film begins by offering the viewer considerable background on the community and Babette's arrival, and then moves forward a number of years to the main action. It focuses on the health of a number of characters, and on the members of the religious community generally, as they come to later stages in their lives. The characters and the community are searching for lost plots; each has made choices that, years later, he or she is now reviewing. In many cases, the choices in part seem to have been made for them. The cast is as follows.

(1) The religious community: under the direction of a charismatic leader long dead, the community came together to attempt to follow their beloved master's teaching. In doing so, they have forsaken "the things of the world," including physical love. As the film opens, the community has become fractured: it is aging, and no children are present to carry on the master's memory; life together over so many years has resulted in many quarrels and hurts, many no longer expressed or even clearly remembered, but the effects of which are still very much present; the community has fallen into legalism, following the customs of the master's teaching, but forgetting its spirit. They reside in a remote corner of Danish Jutland, away from the influences of the greater world.

(2) Philippa and Martina, the master's daughters: these two women became the leaders of the community upon the master's

death, and were referred to by him as his right and left hands. Philippa is a gifted singer. She briefly studied opera under Achille Papin, who had come to Jutland in order to search for meaning in his own life. There, in church, he had heard Philippa's singing, and decided that he had found both a love interest and a new diva—someone through whom he could vicariously reanimate his own opera career. Philippa, however, makes the decision to have Achille sent away and restricts her talents to serving the community. She still thinks of him, though, and one senses that she wonders what life as a diva on the stages of Europe would have given her.

Martina seems to be the more prominent of the two sisters, and she too chose life in the community over that in the broader world. Her opportunity to leave Jutland came through a young general who had been sent to his aunt's home in Jutland to address his behavioral problems and commitment to his career. He chooses to leave Jutland and recommit himself to fame and the life of the royal court. She stays behind and provides leadership, but still thinks about the general. As both Philippa and Martina worry about the future of the community—factions are increasing, and they are not sure how much longer they can physically care for those who have grown weak—Martina wonders if the sacrifice of her leadership has been for nothing.

(3) Lorens Lowenhielm is the general in question, and, having been touched by the master's message as well as by the possibilities of love during his stay in Jutland, he now wonders, as his career nears its end, if he had made the correct decision. What, he wonders, has become of his plot?

(4) Babette was a great Parisian chef, considered an artist in her field, who has lost in France's civil war both her family and a setting in which she may practice her art. Achille Papin writes the sisters, asking them to please give Babette a home. But her

place of exile could not seem more bleak: she lives as a servant to Martina and Philippa, among an ascetic religious community that understands little of "the world" and that has little taste for food beyond its basic form. The great French chef makes simple foods, lives in a culture that is not her own, and has lost so much: her home, her family, the satisfaction of her vocation.

Thus does the film carefully build the crises of its characters, until two unlooked-for twists of plot intervene: the community desires to have a meal together on the occasion of the hundredth anniversary of the minister's birth, and Babette wins the French lottery—a friend at home regularly enters a ticket, and she is suddenly the winner of 10,000 francs.

The Jutland religious community immediately enters panic mode upon receiving these disruptions to their "plot." Martina and Philippa, apparently cognizant enough of the tendencies of lottery winners, assume that Babette will take her winnings and go back to France, leaving them alone to care for the aged of their community. But worse things occur! Babette asks them if she can cook the anniversary meal in honor of the minister (after which they are then certain she will leave), and she insists on paying for it herself and on making it a French dinner. They had just hoped for a "simple meal with some coffee served at the end," but as the supplies arrive, it is clear that Babette has ordered exotic food (quails, a live turtle for the soup) and cases of wine.

To make matters worse for Martina, she learns that Mrs. Lowenhielm and her nephew, the general, will attend the meal as well. She will therefore be tested on several fronts. The anxiety builds so that, the night before the meal, Martina has a dream in which Babette offers her a goblet of wine. The goblet is dropped in front of her, and it contains not wine, but blood. Martina confesses to the community she is afraid that she has become party to a "witch's sabbath," and the community unites around her, promising to eat the meal but to pay no attention to its physical aspects.

In Shakespeare's comedies, in which characters often find that life has lost its sense and seems ready to disintegrate into chaos, there exists a place called a green world. It is usually a forest, a wilderness, in which the laws and rules of the society in question no longer apply. Characters wander into the green world only to have their worlds turned upside down and, in doing so, find their real selves again. In *Babette's Feast,* the meal itself is the green world: a realm in which the participants do not know the rules and are taken out of their comfort zones in order to be transformed. The possibility of a "real French meal" in the middle of the culinary wilderness represents chaos and unfamiliarity to almost all of its participants. The Jutlanders are at a loss as to how one should properly identify this food, much less eat it. One older member of the community appreciatively sips a glass of champagne, and comments that it must be some sort of lemonade.

Such consumption certainly loosens the resolve of the participants. They not only begin to enjoy the food, but they begin to enjoy each other's company. The bickering gives way to a recitation of shared memories of the master's life and teaching. This feast in the wilderness is not just a nourishing respite; Babette has carefully prepared a banquet, filled with skill and generosity.

The great irony here is that Lorens, the outsider, is the one recipient of Babette's gift who can appreciate the art and the spiritual significance of the meal; he shepherds the Jutlanders through the "Eucharist." While they are being both intentionally and unintentionally ignorant of the artistry that has gone into preparing the meal, he instructs the community, by example, on how to eat the food, and he presents a homily on its meaning. As the meal ends, Lorens stands to deliver his soliloquy, in which he tells the stunned participants that the words of their master have become the favorite reading (perhaps, we think, through his own influence) of Her Majesty the Queen. Then Lorens tells the following story:

One day in Paris, after I had won a riding competition, my French fellow officers invited me out to dine at one of the finest restaurants, the Cafe Anglais. The chef, surprisingly enough, was a woman. We were served Cailles en Sarcophage, a dish of her own creation. General Galliffet, who was our host for the evening, explained that this woman, the head chef, had the ability to transform a dinner into a kind of love affair, a love affair that made no distinction between bodily and spiritual appetite. General Galliffet said that in the past he had fought a duel for the love of a beautiful woman. But now there was no woman in Paris for whom he would shed his blood—except this chef. She was considered the greatest culinary genius. What we are now eating is nothing less than Cailles en Sarcophage.

"Mercy and truth have met together. Righteousness and bliss shall kiss one another." Man, in his weakness and short-sightedness, believes he must make choices in this life. He trembles at the risks he takes. We do know fear. But no. Our choice is of no importance. There comes a time when our eyes are opened. And we come to realize that mercy is infinite. We need only await it with confidence, and receive it with gratitude. Mercy imposes no conditions. And, lo! Everything we have chosen has been granted to us, and everything we have rejected has also been granted. Yes, we even get back what we rejected. For "mercy and truth are met together; and righteousness and bliss shall kiss one another."

The stunned attendants look at him with wonder. What is he saying about the meal? About God's love and physical love? Who is this man, whom they remember as a rebellious young military officer, to quote the psalms? The meal ends, as a Eucharist should, as a love feast of reconciliation. The old feuds are dropped, the master's words are remembered and put into action once more within the dying community, so that its members will enter the next life in the condition God wants for them. Lorens and Martina seem to come to an acceptance of their love for each other, not as a lost opportunity, but as something strong and alive that mere time and place cannot destroy. As he prepares to leave, the general shares a moment alone with her and says:

> I have been with you every day of my life. . . . You must also know that I shall be with you every day that is granted to me from now on. Every evening I shall sit down to dine with you: not with my body, which is of no importance, but with my soul. Because this evening I have learned, my dear, that in this beautiful world of ours, all things are possible.

All of this work of God has come through someone who hardly considered herself an agent: Babette. She likely spent considerable time, like Joseph in his own exile, mourning the loss of her family and her homeland, wondering why her talents were withering away or being spent in so unlikely a circumstance on a people who did not seem to appreciate them. To be praised by the general as she was, to be known as the greatest culinary genius in France, must have filled her head with great dreams. How was this plot for her life to be fulfilled in Jutland? How were her talents to be used on a people who expected and preferred dried fish, water, and beer bread for their dinners?

But Babette learns through the use of her gifts, exercised in the strange plot God has devised for her, two extremely countercultural notions familiar to any reader of the New Testament: that we find ourselves in losing ourselves, and that treasure, which will focus the desires of our hearts, is to be stored up in heaven rather than on earth.

At the end of the film, the two sisters, after complimenting Babette in a rather perfunctory manner on the quality of the dinner, fully expect her to return to France. But Babette tells them that she has no money—it was all spent on the preparation of the meal. And she no longer has a life in France; her family is here. Martina and Philippa are stunned at the cost of the meal. Babette does confess that she has experienced the opportunity once again to practice her art, that the meal was not for their benefit only. In response, Philippa, the artist who could have lived out her life as a diva on Europe's great stages, embraces Babette. They say the following words to each other:

> [Philippa:] "Did you prepare that sort of dinner at the Cafe Anglais?"
>
> "I was able to make them happy when I gave of my very best. Papin knew that."
>
> "Achille Papin?"
>
> [Babette smiles.] "Yes. He said, 'Throughout the world sounds one long cry from the heart of the artist: Give me the chance to do my very best.'"
>
> "But that is not the end, Babette, I'm certain of that. In Paradise, you will be the great artist that God meant you to be. Ah, how you will delight the angels!"

I have had to come to the hard conclusion in my own life that moments when I feel that God's plot has been lost are sometimes moments when I am trying too hard to hold on to my own conception of it. To work within the plot I have been given, keeping in mind God's good intentions for me and letting my hope for a good life be inspired by his plans, results in a deepening of me and service to others that would not have been possible if I'd had my way. It also breaks me open—and with that, I begin to love other people. And in this context Lorens's words at the feast ring true for me as well, rather than the hard message I heard from the missionaries in my Christian youth: the mercy that fills this world has no bounds; we get back what we thought we had lost, in ways and to degrees we never could have imagined.

The story of Joseph for me is one of the most poignant in the Bible. It speaks to both hope and apparent despair and, I think, in hope of a future not yet fulfilled. Here is Joseph's conversation with his brothers and then his father's request of him at the end of Genesis:

> And now, do not be distressed . . . because it was to save lives that God sent me ahead of you. . . . So then, it was not you [my brothers] who sent me here, but God. He made me father to Pharaoh, lord of his entire household and ruler of all Egypt. Now hurry back to my father and say to him, "This is what your son Joseph says: God has made me lord of all Egypt. Come down to me; don't delay. You shall live in the region of Goshen and be near me—you, your children and grandchildren, your flocks and herds, and all you have. I will provide for you there . . ." (Gen. 45:5–11)

> . . . promise that you will show me kindness and faithfulness. Do not bury me in Egypt, but when I rest with my fathers, carry me out of Egypt and bury me where they are buried. (Gen. 47:29–30)

I have had to come to the hard conclusion in my own life that moments when I feel that God's plot has been lost are sometimes moments when I am trying too hard to hold on to my own conception of it.

Our stories do not end in this Egypt, in whatever exiles we find in our own lives. For many years I wondered at the following statement by the writer of the New Testament letter to the Hebrews:

Since the children [of God] have flesh and blood, [Jesus] too shared in their humanity so that by his death he might destroy him who holds the power of death—that is, the devil—and free those who all their lives were held in slavery by their fear of death. (Heb. 2:14–15)

I knew that in some sense we believers were not to be afraid of death, although the thought of dying has always had that effect on me. But perhaps, like Babette and like Joseph, we are to realize that the episodes in life that may seem like a death to our dreams bear fruit, and that what God created us to be does not end in this life, but in a life and realm where all will be set right again.

Pastor Rick Warren, author of *The Purpose-Driven Life,* recently stated in one of his sermons:

The body of Christ, unfortunately, has become a big mouth. We have lost our hands and feet. Our culture certainly knows through our words what Christians are against, but it has little idea through our actions of what we are for.

One of the clearer moments of understanding that I believe God gave to me came in an unexpected setting. Our church in Chicago, through the tireless work of a handful of its members, decided to set aside some of its building and grounds for a day-care center. This project would provide a significant number of spaces for young women at the neighboring high school who had had babies, or who were going to have them soon, and who could not finish high school without some help.

By the grace of God, the project took off, and God used it to reach the community. We had amazing stories to tell, such as that of the man who happened to walk into our church one morning because his car broke down—he could not attend his usual congregation miles away. He happened to hear our pastor announce the day-care center's opening. The man waited for our pastor after the service, told his story about the car, and confessed that just yesterday he had been stunned by the news that his high-school-aged daughter was pregnant.

But the project was difficult. It caused divisions within the church, it asked us to commit to spending money that we did not have, and it stretched the church's vision of its identity. The task produced casualties in the congregation, and positive results were not always easy to see. At one point, in a low moment of frustration, a few people complained that we were giving our money away to people who didn't even appreciate it, much less who could ever pay us back. And then it struck us that this is exactly what God did for us.

The identity of the religious community that Babette finds in Jutland had become identified by its mouth—by words that rarely were played out in action, and by a shrinking of that community so that it was no longer even serving its own members, much less others outside the community.

Once Babette's decision is made to use her money to serve those who are in desperate need, but who may not appreciate or repay her kindness, we see Babette's determination in planning the meal, ordering the ingredients, and then carefully preparing the room for the guests and each course of the meal in its turn. She samples wines and sauces as she cooks, but she herself does not eat. Her purpose is the redemption of this community—those loved by God who have taken so many wrong turns and need to be healed of these errors and heartaches before their lives on this earth will end. And so Babette, for me, illustrates in a new way the work of Christ: choosing to humble himself, removing himself from his position of glory to live among us, and healing the brokenhearted and calling us sinners to repentance. And, just as Babette's guests do not understand the work that went into the food and the quality of what they are offered, and just as they do not even fully appreciate the sacrifice made for them, we sometimes take Jesus for granted, or simply do not understand what he gave up. In Babette's rediscovery of her plot in exile, the actions of service speak loudly: she prepares a meal in the wilderness for her fellow wanderers and, in doing so, shows them the way home.

Afterword

This is an inadequate book. Part of its flaw, perhaps, is the nature of the human story itself: our stories are never really finished, our understanding of our own plots is never complete, and though we have a promise that someday God will make all things new again and that our plots will be fulfilled, we live in the here and now of human incompleteness. I think that we have two primary options in addressing this problem. We can pretend that the incompleteness simply isn't so, or we can accept it. As Anne Rice's Jesus states at the end of her novel, we can agree that we have been "sent here to be alive. To breathe and sweat and thirst and sometimes cry."

Please don't take the first option; don't pretend that life's incompleteness isn't so. We have enough people in the world pretending that all is well, and such points of view usually end badly. If you're worried about being a witness to the truth, but not seeming a very attractive witness because of your flaws, or the messiness of your plot right now, then remember Reuben Land's advice in *Peace Like a River*: "No miracle happens without a witness. Someone to declare, Here's what I saw. Here's how it went. Make of it what you will." We cannot cause others to believe. But we can care enough for our fellow travelers to tell the story without having to dress it up. A witness sees and reports; a jury decides.

I was lucky enough to spend some time with my son Eric the other night. He is a teenager now—a little gangly and unkempt, appreciative of sharp wit and irony, and able to utter something that occasionally just puts me on the floor. We were downstairs in his room, watching something together on television and, in our typical family way, multitasking. The atmosphere was relaxed, the conversation casual. I continue to see in him the faint reminders of his condition: an occasional difficulty forming a word he has to use; almost a second-language sound to some of his vowels. Sometimes it hurts me to hear it, and I freeze up a little because—oh, my goodness—it's a sign that the world isn't how it should be. But Eric is well: social, intelligent, tender-hearted, and kind. He may be marked by signs of this world's brokenness, but we are all so marked.

Thank God for signs like these—for Jacob's limp, for Anne Lamott's honesty, for Reuben Land's mistakes, for Joseph's tears shed over his brothers, for Owen Meany's little oddities and his Christlike faith. We look forward, all of us, to the day when God will wipe away every tear; in the meantime, we find a warm fire on a cold night, and we sit down to tell our stories.

Thanks go to many people for helping me with this book, whether they knew it or not. So, thanks to Bud and Audrey Hodgkinson for believing that a small church could build a day-care center, to our book club in Chicago who nursed us through Terry's medical school with conversation and good books—especially to Christine Bertrand who cooked as well as Babette and restored our souls. Thanks to my colleagues in Chicago and California who had faith in my own ability to tell a story; thanks to Rodney Clapp of Brazos for his faith and patience. Thanks to our families for hanging with us through better and worse. Thanks to Jon, Eric, and Kevin for literary conversations and for being the sons I had always dreamed of. I hope that my father, who always wanted to be a writer, can talk with me about this book in heaven. And thanks beyond words to my wife, Dr. Teresa White de Roulet, for loving me. She is my hero.

Works Cited

Axel, Gabriel (director). *Babette's Feast*. Panorama Film A/S, Det Danske Filminstitut, 1988.

Enger, Leif. *Peace Like a River*. New York: Grove Press, 2001.

Irving, John. *A Prayer for Owen Meany*. New York: Ballantine Books, 1989.

Lamott, Anne. *Traveling Mercies: Some Thoughts on Faith*. New York: Anchor Books, 1999.

Ramis, Harold (director). *Groundhog Day*. Sony Pictures, 1994.

Rice, Anne. *Christ the Lord: Out of Egypt*. New York: Knopf, 2005.

Sanes, Ken. *Transparency*. http://transparencynow.com/groundhog.htm. 2006.

Smith, Chuck, Jr., *The End of the World . . . As We Know It*. WaterBrook Press, 2001.

Smith, Lee. *Cakewalk*. New York: Ballantine Books, 1983.

———. "In Her Own Words." http://leesmith.com/bios/words.php. 2006.

———. *Me and My Baby View the Eclipse*. New York: Ballantine Books, 1990.